CHOSEN AND CHERISHED

Chosen and Cherished
BIBLICAL WISDOM FOR YOUR MARRIAGE

Kimberly Hahn

PUBLISHED BY ST. ANTHONY MESSENGER PRESS
CINCINNATI, OHIO

RESCRIPT

In accord with the *Code of Canon Law*, I hereby grant my permission to publish *Chosen and Cherished* by Kimberly Hahn.

Monsignor Kurt H. Kemo
Vicar General
of the Diocese of Steubenville
Steubenville, Ohio
May 1, 2007

The permission to publish is a declaration that a book or pamphlet is considered to be free from doctrinal or moral error. It is not implied that those who have granted the permission to publish agree with the contents, opinions or statements expressed.

Unless otherwise noted, Scripture passages have been taken from the *Revised Standard Version*, Catholic edition. Copyright ©1946, 1952, 1971 by the Division of Christian Education of the National Council of the Churches of Christ in the USA. Used by permission. All rights reserved. (Note: The editors of this volume have made minor changes in capitalization to some of the Scripture quotations herein. Please consult the original source for proper capitalization.)

Cover design: Constance Wolfer
Cover image: Giotto di Bondone, The marriage of the Virgin.
Photo credit: Cameraphoto Arte, Venice / Art Resource, NY
Book design by Phillips Robinette, O.F.M.

LIBRARY OF CONGRESS CATALOGING-IN-PUBLICATION DATA
Hahn, Kimberly.
  Chosen and cherished : biblical wisdom for your marriage / Kimberly Hahn.
      p. cm. – (Life-nurturing love)
  Includes bibliographical references.
  ISBN 978-0-86716-848-8 (pbk. : alk. paper) 1. Marriage—Religious aspects—
Catholic Church. 2. Marriage—Biblical teaching. 3. Bible. O.T. Proverbs
XXX—Criticism, interpretation, etc. I. Title.

BX2250.H34 2007
248.8'44—dc22

                            2007011269

ISBN 978-0-86716-848-8

Published by Servant Books, an imprint of St. Anthony Messenger Press
28 W. Liberty St.
Cincinnati, OH 45202
www.ServantBooks.org

Printed in the United States of America.
Printed on acid-free paper.

    08 09 10 11 5 4 3 2

Contents

Introduction

For fifty years my parents have modeled Christian marriage and family life. They have prayed, studied the Scriptures and applied the lived wisdom offered by those who were ahead of them in the process. In turn they have mentored us: They have shared what they have learned and pointed us in the direction of resources that would encourage us and give us wisdom for particular situations. Mom and Dad have known the deep joy of being chosen and cherished, and their prayer has been that each of their children know that as well, both from the Lord and from their spouses.

Chosen and Cherished is the first in a series of Bible studies on the vocation of marriage entitled *Life-Nurturing Love*. For nearly two decades I have shared these studies with Franciscan University students—married and not yet married—in my home. Based on Proverbs 31 as a kind of table of contents, we range through Scripture and Church teaching for practical applications to the vocation of marriage as well as spiritual applications in our relationship to *the* Beloved, Jesus.

We begin with the Lord because he alone, the Bridegroom of our souls, can fulfill the deepest longing of our hearts. *He* has chosen us, and *he* cherishes us. From that beginning point the Lord invites us to embrace a particular spouse who will be a channel of grace for us—someone who, in imitation of the Lord, chooses us and cherishes us each day.

A marriage built on the foundation of faith is the core relationship of the family. From this relationship we draw strength; from our committed love our children draw strength. Though the demands on our time and energy may be focused on our children, we need to nurture our relationship with our spouse continually, so that our love is ever deepening and enduring.

Spouses and children do not come with manuals, and the learning curve can be very steep, especially for those who did not experience Christian marriage and family life growing up. Still, the Lord has an abundance of grace for each of us. *His* desire is our own: that we be chosen and cherished by our spouses for a lifetime. This Bible study provides biblical wisdom to help us grow in this direction.

Chosen and Cherished is a Bible study presented on DVD and in this book. Either resource stands alone as a study, though the two will be more meaningful when used together. In the back of this book, I have included outlines for the DVD presentations and sets of questions for discussion. Consider reading the entire selection in Proverbs 31 each day, so that you keep the individual verse you are studying in the context of the whole passage.

My hopes are that this study will further the sharing of lived wisdom among generations of women, provide a context in which married couples can better understand some principles of Christian marriage and family life, and enable engaged couples to explore their hopes and dreams for a fulfilling marriage before they are in the thick of it.

Let's pray for each other and encourage each other, remembering the words of Saint Paul, "I can do all things in him who strengthens me" (Philippians 4:13).

Kimberly Kirk Hahn

PART ONE

Who Can Find a Good Wife?
Proverbs 31:10a

CHAPTER ONE

A Woman Who Fears the Lord

Why study Proverbs 31? The first part of the answer lies in why it was written. This passage of Scripture contains instructions from a queen mother to her son, King Lemuel of Massa, advising him of the qualities that he should seek in a wife. This is a unique contribution in Scripture: the only chapter written by a woman.

The queen mother knows her son may be tempted to see a wife as another possession to acquire. She alerts him: Compared to collecting horses or houses or other fine objects, his search for a good wife will be far more difficult, for she is a rare find. The king's mother wants her son to set his standards high, to seek diligently and to select a wife carefully. She knows that his future spouse will make a difference not only in his well-being but also in the well-being of the kingdom. Much weighs in the balance.

Proverbs 31:10–30 not only serves as a standard by which a man may judge a woman worthy of his pursuit, but in turn it offers traits for a woman to develop so that she can be a good wife. It also inspires a young man to develop qualities that would draw such a woman to want to be the queen at his side.

What Does It Mean to Be "Good"?

The queen mother begins with a question, "Who can find a good wife? / She is far more precious than jewels" (Proverbs 31:10). She wants her son to understand that she is addressing something very important, for a good wife is unlike anything else in his experience. She is aware that since he is the king, many women will be tempted to seek him, to parade in front of him, to try to entice him. She wants him to keep his priorities straight, so that he (and the kingdom) will be blessed with a godly queen.

The queen mother is not telling her son to find someone with moral standards: There are upright people who are not women and men of faith. The last verse of this passage puts verse 10 in context: "Charm is deceitful, and beauty is vain, / but a woman who fears the LORD is to be praised" (Proverbs 31:30). Here is a woman who desires the interior beauty of virtue and godliness rather than external beauty and accomplishments (though she may have these as well). Since she lives according to her priorities, eventually she gains the praise of others, beginning with her husband and children. (As a young mother I took great comfort in realizing that her children must be old enough to recognize her worth. Maybe it took her time to develop all of these godly attributes!)

The godly woman is good by God's standards: She possesses moral perfection, which is only possible in

Christ. A woman who fears the Lord is to be praised: Her godly fear leads her to be good. She needs to be a daughter of the King of Kings before becoming wife to the king.

The woman described in Proverbs 31 is a woman of faith, a woman of excellence, worthy of being elevated to the level of an example for all. She has both physical and spiritual strength, and all with whom she has contact benefit from it.

Now, you cannot "make" a man or a woman be good, but you can anticipate goodness from one who is a Christian, because "goodness" is a fruit of the Spirit (see Galatians 5:22–23). "He who finds a wife finds a good thing, / and obtains favor from the LORD" (Proverbs 18:22). A man obtains favor or grace from the Lord when he finds a godly wife, for she is a grace-gift to him. He values a woman with a heart for God because *he* has a heart for God.

The Fear of the Lord

The husband of the Proverbs 31 woman honors his beloved with these words: "Many women have done excellently, / but you surpass them all.... / A woman who fears the LORD is to be praised" (Proverbs 31:29–30). He says the words we long to hear from our spouses and our children: "Well done!" These verses serve as bookends with verse 10, holding together the various thoughts contained in between with the fact that a woman who fears the Lord is indeed desirable.

What does it mean to fear the Lord? It means to have awe and reverence for him. The woman who fears the Lord obeys from a heart of love for the God of the universe, who is also her heavenly Father! Her childlike fear of her heavenly Father leads her to faithful and faith-filled obedience.

Jesus tells us that, when we pray, we are to say "Our Father": His Father is our Father. Through the Son we are drawn into an intimate relationship with the Father. The love the Father has for the Son, Jesus, extends to us. Through Baptism God makes us his children, so our relationship with God is one of a child to the Father.

A child's natural "fear" of his or her father is similar to our supernatural "fear of the Lord": The child looks up to the father with love, respect, admiration and, yes, a certain amount of fear. Likewise we look to our heavenly Father with the kind of awe, worship and adoration that are due the Lord. Our obedience flows from our respect and love.

An image that illustrates this is the famous photo of a very young John F. Kennedy, Jr., playing under his father's desk in the Oval Office. Though his father was president of the United States, the most powerful country in the world, the young John was welcome to play near him. Likewise we are invited to draw near the feet of our Father, who is not a mere president but Lord of the universe! He is approachable and accessible.

How are we to fear the Lord? Psalm 112 gives us the answer: "Praise the LORD! / Blessed is the man who fears the LORD, / who greatly delights in his commandments!" (Psalm 112:1). Like the psalmist, we worship in reverence and joy: The fear of the Lord links joy to obedience.

Our children's obedience gives us a paradigm for our response to our heavenly Father. At first they obey from fear of consequences. That is an acceptable motivator for a young child, especially with safety issues involved. However, we look for the mature love of a child who obeys from the heart—to please us, to honor us. This obedience flows from a proper respect for us.

So it is with God's parenting of us. In the Act of Contrition, we acknowledge that we have offended God, and we repent of our sins because we "dread the loss of heaven and the pains of hell, but most of all because they offend thee, who are all good and worthy of all our love." Fearing the eternal consequences of our actions is an acceptable motivation for our obedience to the Lord—hell does exist—but the mature response God seeks from his children is that they obey because of their love for him.

7

A Flow of Blessings

Many blessings follow fear of the Lord:

> You who fear the Lord, wait for his mercy;
> and turn not aside, lest you fall.
> You who fear the Lord, trust in him,
> and your reward will not fail;
> you who fear the Lord, hope for good things,
> for everlasting joy and mercy.
>
> …
>
> Consider the ancient generations and see:
> who ever trusted in the Lord and was put
> to shame?
> Or who ever persevered in his commandments
> and was forsaken?
> Or who ever called upon him and was overlooked?
> For the Lord is compassionate and merciful;
> he forgives sins and saves in time of affliction.
> (Sirach 2:7–11)

Additional blessings include long life (see Proverbs 10:27; 19:23), riches and honor (Proverbs 22:4). Unlike the fear that leads to despair, godly fear leads to hope: "The LORD takes pleasure in those who fear him, / in those who hope in his steadfast love" (Psalm 147:11).

Proverbs 1:7 states, "The fear of the LORD is the beginning of knowledge." And Proverbs 9:10 echoes, "The fear of the LORD is the beginning of wisdom, / and the knowledge of the Holy One is insight" (see also Proverbs 15:33). Fools despise wisdom and instruction, but a woman who reverences her heavenly

Father desires knowledge and wisdom. This reverence is the first step toward the knowledge and wisdom she needs—and we need—to raise a godly family.

Parenting is continually an adventure into uncharted waters. We learn something with one child that may or may not apply to the next. Our desire for the knowledge and wisdom to have a godly marriage and family is one our Father longs to fulfill. Our desire is his desire for us: Fear the Lord and you will gain wisdom and insight!

Our fear of the Lord has beautiful consequences for our children. "The mercy of the LORD is from everlasting to everlasting / upon those who fear him, / and his righteousness to children's children, / to those who keep his covenant / and remember to do his commandments" (Psalm 103:17–18). Likewise, Mary declares that God's mercy is "on those who fear him / from generation to generation" (Luke 1:50). We set an example for our children; they observe in us the blessings from our fear of the Lord. We train them in obedience so that they will obey God.

The more the fear of the Lord leads us to wisdom, the more we grow in humility. We see who the Lord really is—worthy of our worship—and we see both how small we are *and* how special we are in his eyes. This increases our confidence in the Lord and provides strength for our children. "In the fear of the LORD one has strong confidence, / and his children will have a refuge" (Proverbs 14:26). Our husbands also will have more confidence, and that will translate into our children's growing sense of security and stability: They will have a refuge.

What a contrast with the perspective of the world, whose refrain is "Get more money and your children will feel more secure." Proverbs 15:16 cautions, "Better is a little with the fear of the LORD, / than great treasure and trouble with it." The contrast here is not between great wealth and poverty; the contrast is between having few resources with the Lord versus having wealth (plus the trouble that comes with it) without the Lord. "Only fear the LORD, and serve him faithfully with all your heart; for consider what great things he has done for you" (1 Samuel 12:24).

You Are Mine Twice

I heard this story long ago, and it continues to touch my heart.

One summer a little boy whittled a toy boat. Each day he would float his boat down the stream in his backyard, but one day it got away from him. He searched for it but could not find it.

Toward the end of the summer, the boy was passing the local toy store when he saw, in the window display, *his* toy boat. He immediately went in and told the shopkeeper, but the shopkeeper said that he had paid for it, so the little boy would have to pay for it, too.

Without another word the little boy raced home, broke open his piggy bank, counted his coins and dashed back to the store. He put the money on the counter and ran to the window display. When he reached for the boat, the shopkeeper overheard him say, "Now you're mine twice: First I made you; then I bought you back!"

This is what Jesus says to us, "Now you're mine twice: First I made you; now I've bought you back." This has *always* been the theme of God's love song to his people. (God does not change: he is the same in the Old Testament as in the New.) Through the prophet Isaiah he spoke to his people Israel:

> But now thus says the LORD, he who created you, O
> Jacob,
>   he who formed you, O Israel:
> "Fear not, for I have redeemed you;
>   I have called you by name, you are mine.
> When you pass through the waters I will be with you;
>   and through the rivers, they shall not overwhelm
>   you;
> when you walk through fire you shall not be burned,
>   and the flame shall not consume you.
> For I am the LORD your God,
>   the Holy One of Israel, your Savior.
>   …
> You are precious in my eyes
>   and honored, and I love you.
>   …
> bring my sons from afar
>   and my daughters from the end of the earth,

11

> every one who is called by my name,
>> whom I created for my glory,
>> whom I formed and made." (Isaiah 43:1–4, 6–7)

Saint Paul selects this same theme as he begins Ephesians:

> Blessed be the God and Father of our Lord Jesus
> Christ, who has blessed us in Christ with every spiri-
> tual blessing in the heavenly places, even as he chose
> us in him before the foundation of the world, that we
> should be holy and blameless before him. He destined
> us in love to be his sons through Jesus Christ, accord-
> ing to the purpose of his will, to the praise of his glori-
> ous grace which he freely bestowed on us in the
> Beloved. (Ephesians 1:3–6)

We have been created and destined for his glory. It
does not matter whether your parents intended to conceive you; your loving heavenly Father did. There are
no "accidents." As Ephesians 1:4 states, before the
world was created, our heavenly Father chose you and
me to be created in love. Each one of us has been made
by God, for God—by Love himself, for love. We were
not made in the general sense of humanity but in a
very particular sense, called by name. I tell my children, "Before you were made, you were a loving
thought in the heart of our heavenly Father, who is not
bound by time."

Our heavenly Father has a wonderful plan for each
of our lives. We'll talk about that in the next chapter.

Chapter Two

Trust in the Lord

God created you and me for a purpose. Our destiny is not based on our talents, skills, abilities, gifts, education, wealth or health, though these may be useful. God's plan for our lives *is* based on God's grace and our response to him. All that we have is a gift from God. What we are is a gift back to him.

Ephesians 1:12 states that "we who first hoped in Christ have been destined and appointed to live for the praise of his glory." God's plan is that our lives bring him glory. He has chosen us, in love, to be a living reflection of him. Part of our response to him is our vocation, a particular way of service that allows us to grow in holiness and become more like him.

A Particular Call

Saint Josemaría Escrivá frequently took questions from the audience following a conference. When asked about someone's vocation, Saint Josemaría would inquire if the person was married. If so, he requested the name of the spouse. His response would then be something like, "Gabriel, you have a divine vocation and it has a name: Sarah."[1]

The vocation of marriage is not a general call but a particular call to marriage with a specific person. The spouse becomes an integral part of the other's path to holiness.

Sometimes people have a limited understanding of vocation, using the term only for people called to the priesthood or religious life. But God calls us all to holiness, and the path to that holiness includes a particular vocation. For some the path is single or consecrated life; for many more it is marriage.

In marriage there are many opportunities every single day to deny ourselves, to take up our cross and follow the Lord in holiness. God does not overlook married people! I have days when dinner is late, a child is cranky, the phone rings and rings, and Scott's late getting home. My mind can drift to a scene of nuns praying peacefully in the convent, waiting for the dinner bell to ring. Oh, to be a nun for a day!

I am overwhelmed, caught up in how challenging *my* vocation is. Then I realize that it is no more challenging than any other vocation. It is just more challenging for me, because *this* is God's call on my life. (Numerous nuns have since reassured me that convents are not always the peaceful bliss I picture.)

Marriage to Scott is how God refines me and calls me to holiness; marriage to me is how God refines Scott. We have told our children, "You can pursue any vocation—consecrated, single or married; we will support you in any call. But what is nonnegotiable is that you know the Lord, love him and serve him with your whole heart."

Once two seminarians were visiting, and one of our children waddled through the room with a very full diaper—the odor was unmistakable. One seminarian turned to the other and jokingly said, "I'm sure glad I'm called to the priesthood!"

I immediately shot back (with a smile), "Just be sure you don't choose one vocation to avoid the challenges of the other."

That bit of wisdom applies both ways: One should not choose the vocation of marriage to avoid the challenges of consecrated single life, nor consecrated life to avoid the challenges of marriage. God made each of us for a particular vocation, and there will be great joy in doing what we were made to do. God's call will never be a vocation we do not want. Nevertheless, our vocation will have challenges.

How Does a Protestant Raise a Catholic Child?

Scott became a Catholic about a year and a half before our daughter Hannah was born. As I held her, I was concerned about how I, as a Protestant, would raise her in such a way that she could choose freely the vocation God had for her. I had always envisioned myself training my daughter to be a wife and mother.

But I did not want to be an obstacle if God's plan for her was religious life. My two little boys already had mentioned that they wanted to be priests. How could I guide my children to consider being single for the Lord? (Though Protestants think being single is allowable, they rarely present it as desirable.) I did not want to spoil God's plan; I wanted God's best for them.

So I prayed, Lord, how can I train my children properly to say "yes" to your call on their lives? All of a sudden I realized that mature womanhood *is* spousal commitment and motherhood, and mature manhood *is* spousal commitment and fatherhood. Faithfulness and fruitfulness apply spiritually for all and physically for many.

Living for oneself is not maturity; living for Christ, single or married, is. I understood that if I trained my children to be godly spouses and parents, they would be prepared to choose freely God's call on their lives. I gained an even richer understanding of this when I became a Catholic.

The call to single or consecrated life is not a call to be neutered. In particular, all of the wonderful qualities that are a part of what Pope John Paul the Great referred to as "the genius of women" should be developed in each woman: being hospitable, nurturing, generous, and applying wisdom in relationships, to mention a few. A woman who responds to God's call to the consecrated life does not give up her femininity but rather yields it completely to God as a gift. Likewise, all of the wonderful qualities of manhood can find expression in whatever vocation a man chooses, either for the good of his bride or for the good of Christ's bride, the Church.

A Helper Fit for Him

In Genesis God repeatedly declares, as he examines what he had made, that it is good (see Genesis 1:4, 12, 18, 21, 25, 31). Then he points out something that is *not* good:

> The LORD God said, "It is not good that the man should be alone; I will make him a helper fit for him." So out of the ground the LORD God formed every beast of the field and every bird of the air,…but for the man there was not found a helper fit for him. So the LORD God caused a deep sleep to fall upon the man, and while he slept took one of his ribs and closed up its place with flesh; and the rib which the LORD God had taken from the man he made into a woman and brought her to the man. Then the man said,
> "This at last is bone of my bones
> and flesh of my flesh;
> she shall be called Woman,
> because she was taken out of Man." (Genesis 2:18–23)

God creates a good wife for Adam, a helper fit for him, made from his flesh and bone. Then God awakens Adam and presents to him his bride.

This image of God fashioning Adam's mate and bringing her to him served as a backdrop for a conversation I had with a woman who led the summer program in which I was assisting. I was preparing to return for my senior year at Grove City College romantically unattached. I did not want to panic about whether or not I would find my future husband before graduation, but it was on my mind. I longed to be married, yet I wanted to trust the Lord for the timing.

When I shared my concerns with Sibyl, she reminded me that God did not set Eve loose in the garden and say, "Go find Adam!" Nor did he send Adam to hunt for Eve. Rather, at the right time, God made Eve for Adam and presented her to him. Adam awoke to discover the gift God had given him.

Sibyl assured me that, at the right time, God would present me to my Adam; I would not need to make it happen. For the time being I should let God refine me so that I would become the helper fit for that man, just as he had fashioned Eve.

These wise words from a good friend led me to deepen my trust in the Lord and to pray for that future spouse, whoever he might be, without feeling that I had to find him. I returned for my senior year with a focus on serving the Lord, especially in the ministry of Young Life.

Now, the young man who had recruited me for Young Life the year before was a close friend named

Scott Hahn. Throughout the summer I had experienced a growing sense that he could be "the one," but I tried to keep my focus on praying for him rather than daydreaming about him. I knew he could use the prayer, and this kept my mind on the Lord rather than Scott.

By early fall, however, I had a genuine sense that I was looking at my future husband whenever I saw Scott. I told my roommate about this, even adding that I was not sure if I was in love with him yet. I had a peace I could not explain. I knew I could wait for the Lord to move his heart. Little did I know that he already had told others that he was planning to court me.

Within a month of returning to school, we began our courtship. Three months later, on January 23, Scott asked me to marry him. Eight months later, on August 18, 1979, we began the great adventure of the vocation of marriage.

Marriage Brings Changes

A pastor meeting with a couple mentioned that in marriage the two become one. The fiancé quickly asked, "Which one?"

Like this man, some people fear that marriage will mean loss—of individuality, personality, lifestyle or finances. Some view marriage as a change in domicile, merging tastes and assorted furniture; others are already cohabiting, so even these things do not change much. Some wives adopt the husband's name as the family name; others keep their own last names to retain their independence.

Marriage involves fundamental and profound changes in a couple's relationship, roles and potential. Man and woman become husband and wife. This is a new relationship with a new role to explore. Both husband and wife have the potential of enabling the other to become a father or a mother. Is there a more significant or life-altering decision a man or a woman will make?

Channel of Grace

When Scott prepared to become a Catholic, we wondered whether our marriage would need a special blessing in order to be sacramental. We learned that since we were baptized Protestants when we wed, ours was a sacramental marriage already, though we had not understood what that meant at the time.

My father, the pastor who married us, often reminded us (and still does), "Kimberly, you are now the primary channel of grace for Scott; Scott, you are the primary channel of grace for Kimberly." This fits Catholic teaching beautifully. The road of my sanctification runs through Scott. He is not an obstacle to my sanctification; he is an integral part of my path to sanctity, and I am an integral part of his.

Grace flows from Christ to the Church, and the Church dispenses grace to us his children, giving glory back to Christ. Likewise, in the sacrament of marriage, we become channels of grace to each other and through us to our children, all for the greater glory of God.

Here are some critical questions to ask yourself if you are not yet married: Does the person I'm dating encourage me in my faith, or is he or she a roadblock? Will I be able to assist this person toward holiness, or is he or she resistant to the faith? These questions highlight the importance of a Christian spouse.

A word of caution: Sometimes people assume that it does not matter whether or not a future mate is strong in the faith because the Church permits (with the proper dispensation) a couple to marry even if both are not Christians.

However, permission from the Church does not mean that the Church desires such unions. Choose someone who will share the call to know God, love God and serve God in this life and enjoy him forever. Do not settle for someone who is willing to let you pursue a life of faith by yourself. You need someone who shares your vision of living for God.

Love God With Everything

Everything we have is on loan from God, especially the people in our lives. It is not *our* money, *our* possessions, *our* family! The vocation of marriage is a vocation of

21

stewardship. We are happiest when we live in light of the lordship of Jesus Christ together with our spouse.

Maybe you have set up "No Trespassing" signs around the home of your heart: "Lord, you're welcome in the living room, but don't disturb the library, where I've collected thoughts I want to keep." Or, "You're welcome in the dining room, but please stay out of the bedroom!" Or, "You're welcome in the kitchen, but please keep the pantry door shut. I've stuffed it with things that are rotting, and I'm not ready to clean it yet!"

Jesus responds, "I want to be the LORD of the manor of your heart." He wants to move in, clean and set up his throne. We do not make him Lord; he *is* the Lord. The question is, are we going to acknowledge his lordship in our lives? Are we going to allow him in to clean the dark corners of our hearts?

Sometimes people see themselves as cultural Catholics: The Church is part of their tradition, but it does not play a role in their day-to-day decisions. If the Church is a part of your heritage, that is a great gift. However, a gift has to be opened and used or it has not been received. The Lord asks us to search our hearts about what we believe and what we are willing to live.

When Jesus was asked to summarize the Law and the prophets, he quoted Deuteronomy 6:5–6, "You shall love the Lord your God with all your heart, and with all your soul, and with all your mind.... You shall love your neighbor as yourself. On these two commandments depend all the law and the prophets" (Matthew 22:37, 39–40). We are to *love God* first; his love and acceptance will help us to *love ourselves* as he does, and then he will enable us to *love our neighbors,* which include our spouse, our children, our relatives, our brothers and sisters in the Body of Christ and beyond, to the whole world.

The Lord is not looking for people who can check Sunday Mass attendance off their to-do list. He wants our Mondays, Tuesdays, Wednesdays, Thursdays, Fridays and Saturdays too. He wants *all* of our heart, *all* of our soul, *all* of our strength and *all* of our mind— *all* of us.

It is not enough to recite the Creed; we need to believe it. It is not enough to know the Ten Commandments; we need to obey them from the heart. It is not enough to know our prayers; we must pray. Christ wants to be nothing less than the center of our lives and the center of our marriages.

A Spouse Is a Gift From the Lord

There are some things we can give our children and some things we cannot. "House and wealth are inherited from fathers, / but a prudent wife is from the LORD" (Proverbs 19:14). We can and should pray that each of our children find a godly spouse, but we cannot make it happen. A godly spouse is a gift from God.

If you want a successful marriage—and if you want your children to have successful marriages—it is important to live marriage God's way. He is the one who made us, after all, and he is the one who designed marriage.

This is why the queen mother of Proverbs 31 says to her son, "Do you know how to recognize a good woman for a wife? Listen carefully to know what to value in a wife; then choose wisely."

Likewise, Lemuel needs to be a righteous man. "Many a man proclaims his own loyalty, / but a faithful man who can find? / A righteous man who walks in his integrity— / blessed are his sons after him!" (Proverbs 20:6–7). These men are rare gems. Value them and thank God for them.

So both a woman who fears the Lord and a righteous man are rare finds. They value what God values; they are precious in his sight. They are doing what Saint Paul admonishes the people of Colossae to do: "Set your minds on things that are above, not on things that are on earth" (Colossians 3:2).

My hope and prayer is that throughout this Bible study you will know the pleasure God has in you as his beloved daughter or son. The image on my heart is that of a loving Father who reaches out to you, cups your face in his hands and says, "I love you with all of my heart; love me with all of yours."

If you are married or engaged to marry, trust your

heavenly Father to show you how to live your vocation together in a way that pleases him. Let obedience flow from your loving trust in him. You thus will become more and more the precious gifts you want to be for the Lord and for one another.

If you are unmarried, trust the Lord to guide you to your vocation. Live your singleness in a way that pleases him; do not waste this precious time. Let obedience flow from loving trust in him, and he will continue to unveil his plan for your life. As you pursue godliness, fearing the Lord, you will grow in wisdom, in knowledge and in grace.

PART TWO

Far More Precious Than Jewels
Proverbs 31:10b

CHAPTER THREE

What Really Counts

The word for "jewels" in Hebrew refers to something very costly, like rubies or pearls. Proverbs 31 tells us that these pale in comparison to the value of a godly wife.

In Matthew 13:45–46 Jesus tells about a man who finds a pearl of great price in a field owned by someone else. He puts it back in the ground and then sells everything he has to purchase that field and possess the pearl. The pearl to which Jesus refers is the gospel, worth any price. The Church, possessing the gospel, is a bride of inestimable worth. A similar understanding can be applied to a godly wife: She is worth any amount of sacrifice to her husband and children.

The queen mother knows the king's temptation to consider a wife as a possession, one more thing to get. By highlighting that a wife is far more precious than jewels, she is telling him to keep his perspective. Conversely, her teaching also serves as a reminder to all women to be careful of any man who treats them as a mere possession.

Earlier in Proverbs wisdom is personified as a woman: "She is more precious than jewels, / and nothing you desire can compare with her" (Proverbs 3:15).

As we grow in wisdom, we become more refined in our speech, blessing others with our words. We exemplify the proverb that says, "There is gold, and abundance of costly stones; / but the lips of knowledge are a precious jewel" (Proverbs 20:15). As godly wives and mothers, our wise words are of inestimable value.

The Source of Our Worth

Who or what determines our value? If we look to our present culture, we get one set of answers; if we look to the Lord, we get a very different answer. The world judges us on appearances; God judges the heart.

External criteria include youthfulness, beauty, talent, skill, wealth, intelligence and fame. Though certain individuals excel in these areas, even the "winners" know they stand on shaky ground.

Those with youth or beauty know that it is just a matter of time before someone younger or more beautiful garners attention. Even pageant queens can list flaws they would correct to be more attractive. One attractive but aging actress wondered if she had "the courage" to refuse plastic surgery.

Those with money constantly compare themselves to others with more. How much is enough to be satisfied or to feel secure?

Those with fame—for their physical prowess, skill or talent—wonder how long they will remain in the limelight. And though the rich and famous may appear happy, the papers are replete with stories of their loneliness and isolation.

For some, it is not beauty or brawn that defines them, but their brains establish their sense of worth. They pursue higher levels of education and seek career advancement and its monetary rewards. Yet they know that younger people, willing to be paid less for the same job, are in line waiting for the opportunity. Eventually retirement comes, and then what is left of an identity so closely associated with mental acuity and job performance?

Even marital status can give a false sense of value. Perhaps a woman remains single to prove she does not need a man, only to end up lonely. Or a woman marries in search of an identity, only to discover a sense of loss or abandonment instead of fulfillment. Though our spouses and children should *affirm* our worth, they do not *determine* our worth.

In stark contrast to all of these ways to measure our value, God speaks to the heart of his beloved daughters and sons. He says, *You are precious because I made you and redeemed you. I give you your sense of worth.*

From the Beginning

God created men and women profoundly and wonderfully different, yet both are made in his image. The *Catechism of the Catholic Church* tells us, "God created man and woman *together* and willed each *for* the

31

other" (*CCC*, 371). As Adam affirms, "This at last is bone of my bones / and flesh of my flesh; / she shall be called Woman / because she was taken out of Man" (Genesis 2:23).

The very first command God gives Adam and Eve, which is both a blessing on their marriage and a command, is recorded in Genesis 1:27–28: "So God created man in his own image, in the image of God he created him; male and female he created them. And God blessed them, and God said to them, 'Be fruitful and multiply, and fill the earth and subdue it; and have dominion.'"

From the beginning God draws attention to man as male and female. They are to be a communion of life-giving lovers in imitation of their Triune Lord, in whose image they have been created. When Adam and Eve fall into sin, they are both in need of a Savior. Together they leave the Garden of Eden with the prophecy that a Savior will come (see Genesis 3:15).

Saint Paul makes it clear that, in Christ, there is no distinction between men and women regarding salvation: "For as many of you as were baptized into Christ have put on Christ. There is neither Jew nor Greek, there is neither slave nor free, there is neither male nor female; for you are all one in Christ Jesus" (Galatians 3:27–28).

So men and women are equally made in the image and likeness of God, equally in need of salvation as a consequence of the Fall, equally offered salvation in Christ. Yet men and women are fundamentally different, beginning with the DNA of every cell. Various media bombard us with the contrary notion that, fundamentally, there are no differences between men and women. This idea sets in motion a competitive rather than a complementary relationship. In marriage this false notion encourages men and women toward self-reliance rather than healthy interdependence. This is a misapplication of the truth of the equality between men and women.

Saint Paul cautions, "Do not be conformed to this world but be transformed by the renewal of your mind, that you may prove what is the will of God, what is good and acceptable and perfect" (Romans 12:2). In other words, there are messages of "this world" that are contrary to the will of God. Regarding men, women, the act of marriage, marriage itself and the value of children, how are we conforming to those messages, and how do we need our thoughts to be transformed by the power of the truth?

The Focus Is Service

Our culture characterizes the husband's position as primary provider for his family as a "cultural conditioning" for the purpose of denying women education, careers, prestige and meaningful work. (Besides, just think of what two incomes can mean.) However, God commands men to provide for their families. First Timothy 5:8 warns, "If any one does not provide for his relatives, and especially for his own family, he has disowned the faith and is worse than an unbeliever." Though a wife can assist, the responsibility for the family's financial needs rests on the husband.

Our culture belittles a wife's homemaker role as a cultural ploy to limit women to menial work—childcare, cleaning, cooking—as the unpaid maid. However, Saint Paul addresses the value of this work in calling older women to teach the younger to follow their example of service in the home:

> Bid the older women likewise to be reverent in behavior, not to be slanderers or slaves to drink; they are to teach what is good, and so train the young women to love their husbands and children, to be sensible, chaste, domestic, kind, and submissive to their husbands, that the word of God may not be discredited. (Titus 2:3–5)

A woman's care for her family ennobles her. Even her body reveals that caring for children is primarily her task: Her body makes milk to feed her baby. (No matter what experts say, male lactation will never catch on.) In ways we do not always see, this critical work on behalf of the family in the home bolsters our witness.

God has instilled other differences between the sexes that aid their complementarity. Interpersonally men are more often initiators; women are more often responders. Even in the act of marriage our bodies reflect this: The woman receives the seed from the man.

Men tend to lead with rationality; women tend to lead with emotional sensitivity, and consequently they have a stronger integration of their bodies and emotions. This does not mean that women are irrational and men are emotionally insensitive. But there is a complementarity in the tendency of the man's and woman's responses that enriches their relationship, especially in marriage, when they appreciate each other's perspective.

Likewise, men tend toward knowledge or facts, women toward wisdom and insight. Again, this does not mean that men are foolish and women are unintelligent. But these tendencies balance one another when men and women receive each other's contributions.

Pointing out these differences only becomes offensive when the man's characteristics are seen as having higher value than the woman's. When a man and a woman respect each other, they see the advantages of their differing perspectives. Their complementarity draws them closer to each other, like magnets. They are able to build a healthy, interdependent relationship in courtship that progresses into a godly marriage and a solid family.

Pope John Paul II spoke of the "genius" of woman that is unique, benefiting family first, but also the

Church and culture. He asked women to bring this unique gift to every stratum of society. He also urged women to explore the richness of the unique role of a wife and mother within the home, especially when this role is denigrated by society. He presented the Blessed Virgin Mary as the model of the genius of womanhood in general and of motherhood—physical and spiritual—in particular.

> *Virginity and motherhood co-exist in her:* they do not mutually exclude each other or place limits on each other. Indeed, the person of the Mother of God helps everyone—especially women—to see how these two dimensions, these two paths in the vocation of women as persons, explain and complete each other.[1]

He encouraged women to understand the heart of what it means to be a woman, so that we would know how to serve the Lord as women of God, especially in the vocation of marriage.

A Living Tabernacle

Since men and women are one in Christ, they are temples of the Holy Spirit—living tabernacles. Saint Paul connects the indwelling Holy Spirit with the call to holiness for both men and women: "Do you not know that your body is a temple of the Holy Spirit within you, which you have from God? You are not your own; you were bought with a price. So glorify God in your body" (1 Corinthians 6:19–20).

What price? The price was Jesus' life. How valuable is that?

Our bodies have become the dwelling places of the Holy Spirit. What difference should that make in our manner, dress and conversation?

Behavior fit for a prostitute a century ago now parades across the TV screen: sex with anyone, seductive dress, undignified conversation. In contrast, consider older women you would describe as having godly womanliness. I see in my mother and other older women the following qualities:

- a beauty that is attractive and radiant, not seductive or gaudy
- a demeanor that is well-mannered and dignified
- a disposition that is gentle and mild yet firm and respectful
- a posture that is self-possessed and peaceful rather than frantic
- a manner that is kind, warm and winsome rather than demanding
- a spirit that is sacrificial rather than attention-getting
- an attitude that is lighthearted about things in general while holding convictions deeply
- a heart that is responsive to her spouse and children without being slavish

The list could go on.

Of the women who have been declared saints, which ones incarnate for us the right sense of womanhood? of being a wife? of motherhood? Patrons of mothers include Saints Anne, mother of the Blessed Virgin, and Monica, mother of Saint Augustine. Saint Elizabeth Ann Seton was both a mother and a teacher—a good model for homeschoolers. Saint Gianna Molla gave her life so that her unborn child could live. Consult these and other "older sisters in the faith" for the prayer support you and your family need.

Sexual Purity

How do we glorify God in our bodies? Saint Paul declares, "For this is the will of God, your sanctification: that you abstain from immorality" (1 Thessalonians 4:3). Sanctification refers to the process by which we become holy, like our heavenly Father. "As he who called you is holy, be holy yourselves in all your conduct" (1 Peter 1:15).

In particular Saint Paul links sexual purity with holiness. We may give our sexual purity as a gift to the Lord through consecration as a single person—to serve him with single-minded devotion—or in marriage—to serve him through openness to life. Either way we take the power of our sexuality and give it to the Lord in sacrifice. Purity empowers us to make the gift the Lord desires.

Sexual Impurity

Maybe you were not challenged about sexual purity in religion or Confirmation classes or on retreats. Perhaps you had a parent insist that you use contraception in high school or college. No matter what has happened before now, you need to know the truth so you can live it.

The Lord created the act of marriage for marriage only. In the act of marriage the two become one, and if those two separate and go their own ways, a part of each of them is gone, torn out. Even if they don't know it is sin, there are still consequences: Breaking God's law causes brokenness.

A talk show host was interviewing passersby, asking them if they ever went to bars to "hook up" with someone. One woman quickly responded, "Every weekend."

Taken aback by her definite response, the host asked, "Do you even know their names?"

"That would be much too personal!" she replied. Too personal to know the men's names with whom she was having sex, but not too personal to give herself to them.

We *are* united with someone with whom we experience the act of marriage, no matter what our intentions are. This is not a Hallmark card sentiment, "It's nice to be one with you." It is a metaphysical reality. Even the prostitute, Saint Paul tells us, is united with the man from whom she may want only a paycheck (see

1 Corinthians 6:16). Imagine how sad she becomes, as pieces of her are torn out time and again.

Any act of intercourse between two people who are not married to each other—whether before marriage, during marriage to another or following being widowed or divorced—is a serious sin. Whether or not a couple feel that it is wrong, it is objectively so. They are cut off from a life of grace.

An engaged couple approached their priest to confess the sin of fornication. He responded, "Oh, you're engaged; you're almost married." Thankfully they knew they had sinned and asked for absolution. It was not the priest's prerogative to downplay the seriousness of their sin.

Sometimes people confuse love and lust. Pressure to "make love" does not equal love. Love is self-emptying, self-donating sacrifice for the good of the other. Lust is focused on using the other for pleasure. Love builds trust; lust destroys trust. And trust is foundational for marriage.

Hope From Our Heavenly Father

The prophet Jeremiah brings a message of hope to God's people in exile. They had abandoned true worship of God and seen the glorious temple destroyed. They had witnessed the death of many of their people, including many children. Now, seventy years later, Jeremiah proclaims, "I know the plans I have for you, says the LORD, plans for welfare and not for evil, to give you a future and a hope" (Jeremiah 29:11).

This is a message for us all: Do not focus on fears, failures or weaknesses but on God's love, forgiveness and healing power. He has a plan for a hope-filled future for all of us!

Saint Peter uses the metaphor of construction. Christ is the chosen and precious living cornerstone, rejected by others but prized by his heavenly Father. We also are living stones, chosen and precious. God has redeemed us to be "a chosen race, a royal priesthood, a holy nation, God's own people" (1 Peter 2:9). These are images the Old Testament used to describe God's people (see, for example, Deuteronomy 11:15; Isaiah 43—44). Now Saint Peter applies these phrases to the Church, including us. Our preciousness is not based on what we have or on what we have done but rather on who we are in Christ.

What If You Feel Tarnished?

Purity matters, but whether or not you have retained your purity, *you* are still a gift. You can experience a kind of secondary virginity by choosing to live from this moment on in the purity of lived forgiveness. "Chastity is about the present and the future."[2]

Father B. handed out sealed envelopes to parishioners as they entered the church one Sunday. During the homily he invited people to open the envelopes.

Everyone had two pennies—one shiny and new and one that showed much wear. Father pointed out that though one penny was in much better shape than the other, each had the same value. In the same way, whether clean or tarnished, we all have great worth in the eyes of the Lord.

Perhaps you did not regard your own preciousness enough to wait for marriage before entering into the act of marriage. Or perhaps you have given yourself to someone in adultery. Where do you go from here?

Regardless of the choices you have made before now, the good news is that God can heal and forgive. Whether or not you *feel* precious, God says that you *are* precious because he made you and he is redeeming you.

Now you have a choice: Will you let the feelings of guilt and shame lead you to repentance, so that you can be a forgiven child of God with a new beginning? Or will you ignore the pangs of guilt because you think sexual purity no longer is possible? Remember Jeremiah's words. Now take advantage of the grace the sacrament of Confession offers.

A Sacrament of Healing

We can glimpse the effects of God's forgiveness in Confession by looking at a pearl. A pearl is made by sand that gets inside an oyster and irritates it, so that the oyster produces a casing around the sand. The longer the sand is irritating the oyster, the more beautiful and the larger the pearl becomes.

This is a picture of how the Lord can use even the bad choices we have made. Through Confession we are reconciled to God. Though there are ongoing irritations—consequences of our sins—these represent opportunities for our purification, opportunities for us to be made more beautiful by grace.

We bring our sins to the foot of the cross in Confession. We leave with forgiveness, renewed, with the strength to resist future temptations and the opportunity for penance to heal, in part, the damage our sins have done to the body of Christ. We come tarnished; we go forth restored.

A friend who led a wild life before coming to faith went to Confession. Though she had confessed her sins and received absolution, she still felt guilty. So she confessed the same sins again. When she confessed the sins a third time, the priest asked, "Why are you confessing this again?"

She said, "I feel so bad, so dirty. I don't know how to get rid of it."

He replied, "You already have. Now you are being presumptuous."

"What do you mean?" she reacted. "I thought I was being humble."

"This is not humility," he said gently. "If God Almighty can forgive you, who are *you* not to forgive you?"

My friend left the confessional determined to walk in the knowledge that the past was behind her: She was forgiven! Now she tells others to embrace the humility that can result from humiliation. In fact, pride from remaining sexually pure before marriage can be more harmful to a relationship than humility from repentance following sexual sin. Either way, God's grace is necessary for a relationship to thrive.

What freedom we enjoy as daughters of our heavenly Father! What a blessing to marry a man who also enjoys the freedom that comes with the discipline of Confession (see Psalm 119:9–11). For those of us with sons, the more we can help them establish a habit of Confession, the more we will bless our future daughters-in-law and grandchildren. Likewise, a habit of Confession will bless our daughters and their future families. We can truly inspire each other to keep the channel of grace unobstructed so that, from generation to generation, our family will know the Lord.

CHAPTER FOUR

A Woman of Worth

Saint Luke records that a woman, traditionally identi-
fied as a prostitute, enters the home of Simon, a
Pharisee, who is hosting Jesus. The Pharisee has offered
Jesus neither a foot washing nor a kiss in greeting,
common acts of hospitality. In contrast, this woman
washes Jesus' feet with her tears, dries them with her
hair, then kisses and anoints them with ointment.

Simon observes Jesus to test his authenticity as a
religious leader: Does Jesus know what kind of woman
is touching him? Simon's attitude and actions show his
failure to live his faith well. The sinful woman, on the
other hand, shows her great faith and love. Such is
Jesus' appraisal of the situation:

> Then turning toward the woman he said to Simon, "Do
> you see this woman? I entered your house, you gave
> me no water for my feet, but she has wet my feet with
> her tears and wiped them with her hair. You gave me
> no kiss, but from the time I came in she has not ceased
> to kiss my feet. You did not anoint my head with oil,
> but she has anointed my feet with ointment. Therefore
> I tell you, her sins, which are many, are forgiven, for
> she loved much; but he who is forgiven little, loves

little." And he said to her, "Your sins are forgiven....
Your faith has saved you; go in peace." (Luke 7:44–48,
50)

This woman's sorrow for her sins is her gift to Christ.
He takes the brokenness of a prostitute and forgives
her with the depth of his unconditional love and grace.

Like the woman in this passage, we approach the
sacrament of Confession and pour out our sorrow,
which becomes our gift to the Lord. He receives that
gift, and through the priest he says to each one of us
what he said to her, "Your sins are forgiven. Go in
peace." He cannot take away our sense of regret, but
he can take away our guilt through the sacrifice of
the cross.

Traditionally, the sinful woman has been associated
with Mary Magdalene who is *Saint* Mary Magdalene.
Although there is no positive scriptural identification
of this woman as Mary Magdalene, because of this
association she has for centuries been invoked by those
who struggle with sexual sin. If you are among those,
you might consider adopting Mary Magdalene as a
patron saint. Just think how much love and compassion she has for you. At the same time she will challenge you to believe you are forgiven and to walk in
that great, great love that you have for the Lord. For "if
we confess our sins, he is faithful and just, and will

forgive our sins and cleanse us from all unrighteousness" (1 John 1:9).

Imagine Saint Mary Magdalene quoting the psalmist:

> For God alone my soul waits in silence,
> for my hope is from him.
> He only is my rock and my salvation,
> my fortress; I shall not be shaken.
> On God rests my deliverance and my honor;
> my mighty rock, my refuge is God. (Psalm 62:5–7)

God reestablishes our honor. He *is* our honor!

Pursue Purity

"Shun immorality. Every other sin which a man commits is outside the body; but the immoral man sins against his own body" (1 Corinthians 6:18). Another translation renders this verse, "Flee fornication."[1]

Fornication is sex before marriage. Fleeing fornication does not mean setting a line and then seeing how close you can get to that line without going over. Rather, fleeing is your response to an enemy ready to attack: Run for your life!

A fire in a fireplace provides warmth, light and a wonderful atmosphere; outside the fireplace fire wreaks havoc, causing pain, destruction and death. If a building is on fire and someone yells, "Flee!" your question will not be, "How close can I get without getting burned?" You will run from harm's way.

Marriage is like the fireplace. Sexual intercourse within marriage is holy and good and wonderful; outside marriage it is dangerous. The writer of Proverbs says of adultery:

Can a man carry fire in his bosom
    and his clothes not be burned?
Or can one walk upon hot coals
    and his feet not be scorched?
So is he who goes in to his neighbor's wife;
    none who touches her will go unpunished.
    (Proverbs 6:27–29)

The Catholic Church urges us to avoid the near occasions of sin, those situations that lower our inhibitions and weaken our will to pursue purity. It is not too late to change habits. Here are some tips for unmarried people:

- *Avoid being alone with someone of the opposite sex late at night.* After midnight seems to be a more vulnerable time than before midnight.

- *Avoid activities involving alcohol,* since alcohol can lower your inhibitions. Even a small amount can keep you from thinking clearly.

- *Be on guard whenever you are alone with someone,* especially in an empty apartment or college bedroom. Be realistic: There are temptations to express love physically in a way that is only appropriate in marriage.

- *Talk as a couple about what limits to set* on the physical expression of love before marriage. The Church admonishes us not to engage in actions that stir up desires that only the act of marriage can fulfill. If you arouse the other person in a way that cannot be satisfied yet, you defraud him or her. That leads to frustration and harms the relationship.

- *Setting realistic limitations* helps you hold each other accountable. Some couples have increased their accountability by inviting parents or a close friend to ask them periodically how they are doing in this area.

- *Pray for each other;* however, be careful about times of intense prayer alone together. That may seem laughable, but when you bare your soul before the Lord with someone, you express intimacy, and sometimes this can lead to temptations to be physically intimate. Some priests caution couples to pray with a group or near others, after Mass or in a chapel, rather than pray alone.

- *Establish a regular discipline of Confession.* This is a very helpful means of accountability.

Guard your heart and seek to honor the one you love. Remember: The physical side of a relationship can catch up very quickly to other areas of the relationship.

Focus on building a strong friendship through growing spiritually, sharing intellectually and having fun together. This develops the foundation of a lifelong partnership in marriage. If you do not marry, you will not have regrets, as long as your goal is to honor each other.

Vessels of Beauty

Saint Paul speaks of vessels God has made for his glory:

> Has the potter no right over the clay, to make out of the same lump one vessel for beauty and another for menial use? What if God, desiring to show his wrath and to make known his power, has endured with much patience the vessels of wrath made for destruction, in order to make known the riches of his glory for the vessels of mercy, which he has prepared beforehand for glory? (Romans 9:21–23)

We are those vessels of beauty: vessels of mercy that bring honor and glory to the Lord. He is the potter, and he is fashioning us into something beautiful for him. This is God's work in us, a work in progress. "For we are his workmanship, created in Christ Jesus for good works, which God prepared beforehand, that we should walk in them" (Ephesians 2:10).

Ruth is a wonderful example of a vessel of beauty. Hers is a book well worth reading. Here is a brief summary.

A Jewish family immigrates to Moab in order to

escape a famine in their hometown of Bethlehem. Naomi and her husband permit their two sons to marry Moabite women, Ruth and Orpah. Then calamity strikes: The father and both sons die. Naomi is left with no spouse, no children, no grandchildren and two pagan daughters-in-law in a foreign land.

Though it will be humiliating, Naomi decides to return to her people alone. She releases her daughters-in-law from any obligation to help her and urges them to remarry among their own people. Orpah agrees and leaves, but Ruth clings to Naomi. "Your people shall be my people," she says, "and your God my God" (Ruth 1:16).

Ruth returns with Naomi to a land whose language and customs she does not know. She is peering in from outside Naomi's religion, yet she is willing to enter this world of her mother-in-law because her heart has turned toward the Lord. Naomi is bereft of all she holds dear except for her faith; Ruth is willing to leave all she knows behind so that she can have the faith Naomi has.

When they arrive in Bethlehem, Naomi tells Ruth of the Jewish custom allowing the poor to glean grain: when a farmer harvests a field, he has to round the corners, leaving the corners for the poor. And he can only harvest once, so the poor can glean the remaining wheat. Naomi knows that an older distant relative,

Boaz, has a huge field where it will be safe for Ruth to glean.

Ruth obediently follows Naomi's instructions and works very hard. Boaz notices her and hears about how godly she is. He says to her, "All my fellow townsmen know that you are a woman of worth" (Ruth 3:11).

Naomi explains another Jewish custom, the Levirate Law, to Ruth: A male relative of a deceased husband can request that the widow become his wife to raise up offspring for the deceased man. Though Boaz is much older than Ruth—twice he refers to her as "daughter"—Ruth responds to his claim of kinship and marries him. This is a great example of marital commitment to last a lifetime versus physical attraction without virtue.

Favor From the Lord

The book of Ruth shows how God blesses those who trust in him. Each member of the family—Ruth, Naomi and Boaz—receives favor from the Lord. And the favor extends to all followers of Jesus through them.

Ruth and Boaz have a child, Obed, who becomes the father of Jesse, the father of King David. Though Ruth was born outside the covenant family line, through faith she becomes the great-grandmother of King David. She is one of the few women listed in Jesus' genealogy (see Matthew 1:5–6). The Lord blesses her faithfulness.

Ruth loves her mother-in-law, trusts her word and embraces faith through her witness. Ruth brings honor to the family name and bears an heir who is the absolute delight of Naomi in her old age. This is a witness to the relationship that is possible between a mother-in-law and a daughter-in-law, even after the death of the son and spouse.

Naomi, deprived of everything but a foreign daughter-in-law and her faith, lives to experience the joy of being a grandmother to Obed and being included in the household of Boaz. The Lord restores her honor. The women of Bethlehem proclaim to her about the child: "Blessed be the LORD, who has not left you this day without next of kin; and may his name be renowned in Israel! He shall be to you a restorer of life and a nourisher of your old age; for your daughter-in-law who loves you, who is more to you than seven sons, has borne him" (Ruth 4:14–15).

Boaz, a very upright, godly man, obtains favor from the Lord when he receives Ruth as his wife. Given that he is old, he might not otherwise have married. "He who acquires a wife gets his best possession, / a helper fit for him and a pillar of support" (Sirach 36:24).

Boaz knows the truth of the proverb: "A good man obtains favor from the LORD.... The root of the righteous will never be moved. / A good wife is the crown of her husband" (Proverbs 12:2–4). God establishes the root of the righteous through Ruth and Boaz, as they become part of the direct lineage of King David and Jesus.

Marriage: God's Idea

Jesus is the fulfillment of God's promises to his people in the Old Testament, pledges of faithful spousal love even in the face of Israel's unfaithfulness. But even more, Jesus elevates marriage to a new level, to that of a sacrament. He not only invites his people to be his bride, the Church; he also calls each of our marriages to be a witness to the world of the relationship he has with his bride. After Saint Paul quotes the same passage Jesus quotes (Genesis 2:24), he says, "This is a great mystery, and I mean in reference to Christ and the Church" (Ephesians 5:32). Here the Greek word for mystery, *musterion,* is translated into the Latin *sacramentum,* from which we get the English word *sacrament.*

Vatican II tells us that the sacrament of Matrimony reaches beyond the two people who are in love, as a testimony to God's love for his people. This is God's design as the author of marriage.[2]

In Christian marriage, two persons contribute not only to the well-being of their children but also to the common good of society. Our laws must reflect these realities. We need to promote, preserve and protect the institution of marriage, always remembering that marriage is God's idea.

Many people want to redefine marriage and family because they think people created marriage and family arrangements in the first place. Even in religious circles Christians seeking to be "culturally relevant" issue statements of support for cohabitation and gay marriage. Some Christians seem to think that if their denomination declares something to be true, it will be! But that is as silly a notion—and as dangerous—as having Congress repeal the law of gravity. They not only cannot; but if they try to prove they have, they will be broken by it. Christians who think they have repealed the laws of marriage actually cease to be prophetic and merely echo their culture's dying strains.

Advice for the Lord's Beloved

If you are not yet attached, delight in being the beloved of God. Let his love satisfy you. Rejoice in feeling treasured by him. This will help you know the right guy, too, because he will imitate his heavenly Father in treasuring you! Do not settle for less.

You are a gift to God and to your future spouse. If you have not met that one particular person, and you believe you are called to marriage, this is a time for God to refine you. Pursue godliness and entrust the future to the Lord.

It is not advisable to date a non-Christian. He may be a good guy, a nice guy; but if his heart does not belong to the Lord, do not give your heart, which does belong to the Lord, to him. You may think you are strong enough to be with a non-Christian and not fall in love with him. However, you are forgetting how entangled your heart can become when you spend time with someone.

Do not date someone to convert him. Even if you are sure it would be in his best interest to become a Christian—and it is—you must not trespass on the precincts of his free will. You risk confusion in his heart and mind between making a commitment to you and making a commitment to the Lord. You also presume on the work of the Holy Spirit in this person's life.

How many people have joined the Catholic Church or agreed to get married in the Church just to placate a Catholic whom they loved, only to question the decision or to challenge it later in life? Some have gone so far as to denounce the faith they embraced and to tell their children that the believing parent is lying to them.

Keep in mind that you should unite with someone who sees you as precious the way the Lord does. Does he hold you in high esteem? Are you a rare find for him? Are you dear to him as his beloved? This is how Jesus sees you and how your spouse should value you.

Sometimes people misinterpret the Church's allowance for a Christian to marry a nonbeliever as an admission that this is just as good as marrying a Christian. Though licit, a marriage between a Christian and a non-Christian cannot be a sacramental marriage. Though allowable by dispensation, this arrangement falls far short of the desire of our Lord and the Church for you.

Saint Paul speaks powerfully to this: "Do not be mismated with unbelievers. For what partnership have righteousness and iniquity? Or what fellowship has light with darkness?" (2 Corinthians 6:14). All that we have and are belongs to the Lord; how can we give ourselves to someone who does not also belong to the Lord?

Further, we need all of the grace we can get to have a marriage that flourishes rather than languishes. Another translation renders *mismated* as "unequally yoked."[3] The word picture is that of two oxen that are yoked, but the yoke rests unevenly on their shoulders. Their efforts in pulling will be less productive, and they may pull against each other. They cannot plow together, so they cannot help each other accomplish the task before them.

Why would we want a marriage that cannot tap into the sacramental graces available in marriage because our spouse is not abiding in the source of grace, Jesus? We need more than a spouse who permits us to practice the faith and to teach it to the children. We need a spouse who will encourage us in the faith, who will come alongside us at Mass, who will support our efforts to raise godly children. The deepest longings of our heart are not only to share this life in marriage but also to share eternal life with our families in heaven.

Besides raising concerns about marriage to a non-believer, the *Catechism* cautions about marriage between a Catholic and a non-Catholic Christian. Though "difference of confession between the spouses does not constitute an insurmountable obstacle for marriage,…the spouses risk experiencing the tragedy of Christian disunity even in the heart of their own home…. The temptation to religious indifference can then arise" (*CCC*, 1634). Spouses of different denominations can be tempted to put religion on the back burner rather than try to have a Christ-centered home. And children can be led to believe that if Mommy and Daddy do not talk about religion, then it must not be that important.

So I suggest people date Catholic believers—strong Catholic believers. You need more than someone with a Catholic pedigree: You need someone who understands the faith and wants to keep growing in it. When both people draw closer to the Lord, they draw closer to each other and discover God's beautiful design for marriage. The goal is not to survive but to thrive, to have the best marriage possible.

Just as Christ cleanses the Church "by the washing of water with the word" (Ephesians 5:26), so a faithful husband should cleanse his bride with the washing of the water of the Word. Is your husband or boyfriend helping you become more and more beautiful in the Lord? Does he know the Word of God well enough to be able to help you apply it to your life?

Sometimes we think too little of ourselves and of the witness our marriages can be. Or we fall into the sin of thinking too much about ourselves and our own needs, wants and desires in a selfish way. Either approach can limit us from being all that the Lord wants us to be. We have been blessed to be a blessing not only to our own families but also to our nation and our world. Only God knows the extent to which he will use us. What he is really looking for is our availability and our faithfulness to do whatever he calls us to do.

Are You Married to a Nonbeliever?

If you are already married to a nonbeliever, living the truth will probably have a greater impact than talking a lot about your faith. Saint Peter refers to husbands who became believers through their wives' behavior, rather than through words:

> Likewise you wives, be submissive to your husbands, so that some, though they do not obey the word, may be won even without a word by the behavior of their wives, when they see your reverent and chaste behavior.... Let [your adorning] be the hidden person of the heart with the imperishable jewel of a gentle and quiet spirit, which in God's sight is very precious. (1 Peter 3:1–2, 4)

What does it take for a jewel to be perfectly set? It takes rubbing, polishing, chipping off corners, cleaning and setting in a place where others can see its beauty. God has a lot of work to do in us, to refine us.

Notice that Saint Peter does not link a wife's submission to how godly her husband is. Rather he says that regardless of a husband's faith or lack of it, a wife's reverent actions speak louder than words to call a man to be the man God created him to be. For those of you with non-Christian husbands, this passage highlights the most effective way to draw his heart to the Lord: Do not look for ways to win arguments, but instead develop a quiet and gentle spirit. You are a grace gift from the Lord to your husband, as a blessing of the New Covenant, even if he does not understand the faith.

In ancient Israel, when someone touched a dead body, he or she was declared unclean for a period of time, but when Jesus touches a dead body, power goes forth to resurrect that person (see Numbers 5:2; Matthew 9:25; 11:5; Luke 8:54). In the Old Testament a leper was unclean until a priest gave the all clear, but when Jesus touches lepers, his healing power makes them whole (Leviticus 14; Matthew 8:3; Mark 1:41). And according to Levitical Law, when someone touched a woman with an issue of blood, that person was unclean for a designated time; but when Jesus is touched by the woman with an issue of blood, healing power from him fills her body and stops her bleeding (Leviticus 15:19; Mark 5:25–34). In each case Jesus is not made unclean, but the one who is unclean is restored. Grace is powerful in its effects.

Jesus demonstrates his power by reversing the effects of touching what, under the old covenant, was unclean and making it clean. This is the backdrop for understanding Saint Paul's teaching regarding marriage between a Christian and a non-Christian:

> If any woman has a husband who is an unbeliever, and he consents to live with her, she should not divorce him. For the unbelieving husband is consecrated through his wife, and the unbelieving wife is consecrated through her husband. Otherwise, your children would be unclean, but as it is they are holy. (1 Corinthians 7:13–14)

Saint Paul highlights the power of grace at work through the believing spouse toward the unbelieving spouse and their children. They become holy—that is, they are set apart in a special way for the Lord. This does not mean that they are saved; however, the believing spouse *is* a channel of grace in their lives. And this grace is powerful in its effects on the whole family. Just as Naomi's witness drew Ruth's heart to the Lord, we can allow our love for God to open our loved ones' hearts to him.

PART THREE

The Heart of Her Husband
Trusts in Her
Proverbs 31:11a

CHAPTER FIVE

Foundation of Faithfulness

The prophet Jeremiah says, "The steadfast love of the LORD never ceases, / his mercies never come to an end; / they are new every morning; / great is your faithfulness" (Lamentations 3:22–23). The Lord's love never wavers; his grace knows no bounds. Every day he is completely trustworthy. He provides the foundation of faithfulness on which we build our lives and our families as his faithful and faith-filled children. Even during times of difficulty, we can say with the psalmist, "I will sing of your mercies, O LORD, for ever; / with my mouth I will proclaim your faithfulness to all generations" (Psalm 89:1).

Faithfulness and Trust

"The heart of her husband trusts in her" (Proverbs 31:11a). What does that mean? First of all, it does not mean that she offers him a heart-healthy diet. *Heart* refers to the mind, the soul, the spirit of this man. He entrusts his well-being to her.

He commends himself to one worthy of that trust. The psalmist has duly warned him: "It is better to take refuge in the LORD / than to put confidence in man. /

It is better to take refuge in the Lord / than to put confidence in princes" (Psalm 118:8–9). He does not trust his wife instead of the Lord; rather, he trusts her because she trusts the Lord.

During the time I sensed that Scott was to be my husband, but we were not yet dating, Psalm 37:3–5 was a powerful word for me:

> Trust in the Lord, and do good;
> > so you will dwell in the land, and be nourished
> > > in safety.
> Take delight in the Lord,
> > and he will give you the desires of your heart.
> Commit your way to the Lord;
> > trust in him, and he will act.

My security rested in the Lord, trusting in him to act in his time. In the meantime I focused on doing good and delighting in him. That way I could ask him to either change the desires of my heart or give me what my heart desired. One of those desires was a faithful spouse. Isn't that a good desire?

Love Has Boundaries

I once had a professor who prided himself on causing a ruckus. He opined, "If your spouse does *not* have an affair in the first five years of marriage, it means you have an unhealthy marriage. It means that you don't trust your spouse to be with someone else and return to you."

Faithfulness, according to this professor, equaled stagnation and distrust; unfaithfulness revealed a healthy marriage. What a convoluted view! Some girls left the class in tears; I was ready for a fight.

I approached the professor. "I don't believe you. I intend to marry a Christian who will have the Holy Spirit. As much as he loves me the day we marry, I believe that his love and his faithfulness will grow, for faithfulness is a fruit of the Spirit. Temptations are out there for both my future husband and me to commit adultery, but that doesn't mean we will fall. By the grace of God we'll imitate God's faithfulness by our own."

The professor smirked in response, but Scott and I have lived the truthfulness of these words.

Love has boundaries in marriage, and the health of a marriage is found within those boundaries. We give ourselves completely to one another and to no other. Therein lies freedom and security.

If you are unmarried, realize that past sexual relationships can weaken the trust a future spouse will have in you. Establish chastity as the way you live now, and trust will grow. Use wisdom in sharing about sins of the past: Details are not necessary or helpful. And give your future spouse time to grieve, if he needs to, for the loss of what you have given away. If he is unable to forgive you and grow beyond your past, he is not the one for you. Likewise, if you cannot let him share his past failure and forgive him, then you are not the one for him. Unconditional love is necessary for any marriage to work.

Faithfulness in courtship is important because you are developing the habits for a successful marriage. Privately you give each other no cause for suspicion. For instance, your friends of the opposite sex should also be friends with your beloved. If not, pull back from those relationships so that their intimacy is never misconstrued as unfaithfulness.

Publicly you do nothing that could reflect poorly on the other. You are aware that you represent the other, and you do all you can to honor him or her in front of others.

Missteps Toward Unfaithfulness

When a couple marries they usually do not intend to commit adultery. So how does this ultimate betrayal happen?

The Book of Proverbs gives a scenario of how infidelity unfolds. Let's look at what the seductress does to entice the man and examine the missteps the man takes. Then we'll contrast those actions with what the woman and man of God can and should do. (Warning: Women can have loose morals; men can be stupid.)

For at the window of my house
    I have looked out through my lattice,

and I have seen among the simple,
    I have perceived among the youths,
    a young man without sense,
passing along the street near her corner,
    taking the road to her house
in the twilight, in the evening,
    at the time of night and darkness.

And behold, a woman meets him,
    dressed as a harlot, wily of heart.
She is loud and wayward,
    her feet do not stay at home;
now in the street, now in the market,
    and at every corner she lies in wait.
She seizes him and kisses him,
    and with impudent face she says to him:
"I had to offer sacrifices,
    and today I have paid my vows;
so now I have come out to meet you,
    to seek you eagerly, and I have found you.
I have decked my couch with coverings,
    colored spreads of Egyptian linen;
I have perfumed my bed with myrrh,
    aloes, and cinnamon.
Come, let us take our fill of love till morning;
    let us delight ourselves with love.
For my husband is not at home;
    he has gone on a long journey;
he took a bag of money with him;
    at full moon he will come home."

With much seductive speech she persuades him;
    with her smooth talk she compels him.

All at once he follows her,
> as an ox goes to the slaughter,
or as a stag is caught fast
> till an arrow pierces its entrails;
as a bird rushes into a snare;
> he does not know that it will cost him his life.
> (Proverbs 7:6–23)

The Seductress

The seductress is "wily of heart." She notices that her husband is leaving town with a lot of money—he is not returning home for a fortnight. Now is her opportunity to pursue an affair.

She leaves her house dressed provocatively, intending to lure a man. Rather than remain busy at home, she is wayward and she is loud, fickle and unruly.

She lies in wait in a kind of ambush—her infidelity is premeditated. When she sees the man approach, she is inappropriately affectionate with him.

She speaks to the man seductively yet includes a reference to religious acts she has completed that day, giving a spiritual veneer to her speech. She does not intend to take no for an answer. "For the lips of a loose woman drip honey, / and her speech is smoother than oil; / but in the end she is bitter as wormwood, / sharp as a two-edged sword" (Proverbs 5:3–4).

If the man is married, her enticements may be a kind of competition with his wife: "See how I have prepared to make love with you while your wife does not." She is presenting a challenge, knowing that once a couple has been married for a while, a wife may not tune in to her husband's needs in the same way she did when they first married. She takes advantage of the fact that the wife may be caring for children all day, working at home and possibly juggling work outside the home. She knows that the many responsibilities and pressures of married life can diminish the time, energy and desire for making love.

The adulteress, on the other hand, has no one to think of besides herself and the one she is seducing. A woman who is bent on seducing a man is probably going to take more time to make lovemaking seem really wonderful, really fun, adding all the perfume and luxurious trappings.

The seductress appeals to love: "Come, let us take our fill of love till morning." Is this love? No, this is lust. This is not true commitment; it is each one using the other.

The Man's Lack of Discipline

Notice that the man does not avoid the near occasion of sin. He chooses to go out at night, when he should be home with his family, and deliberately takes the path near the house of the seductress. He can tell himself that he did not pursue her, though he goes where he is sure she will find him. Then he pauses to listen to her. He offers no rebuke when she is affectionate. He lingers as she allays his fears of being found by her husband. He lets her woo him with promises of delight, confusing lust with love.

Instead of being a leader and refusing to enter into sin with the adulteress, he follows her like "an ox to slaughter." No excuse can warrant his actions—not a mid-life crisis, stress at home nor a neglectful wife. Those excuses explain how a man becomes vulnerable, but they do not justify adultery.

For a little bit of pleasure, the cost is tremendous. This is mortal sin, and it will cost him his life. "He dies for lack of discipline, / and because of his great folly he is lost" (Proverbs 5:23). This is of course true for the adulterous woman as well.

What Should a Godly Wife Do?

In contrast to the adulteress, a godly wife wears attractive but modest clothing; she dresses to please her husband rather than to tempt other men. She makes her home a haven where her husband wants to be with her and the family. She has "a gentle and quiet spirit" (1 Peter 3:4). Her speech and affections are sincere and full of love. She practices the faith sincerely rather than as a pretense.

The godly woman prepares for times of intimacy, letting her husband know her joy in physical expressions of love and her desire to meet his needs. She is trustworthy whether her husband leaves town on business or not. She is watchful, aware that temptation might come but not living in fear and suspicion toward her spouse. She prays for herself and her spouse regularly for protection against any evil that would rob them of the security and happiness of their marriage and family.

What Should a Godly Husband Do?

The man's solution to the lure of adultery is to fill his heart with delight in the wife of his youth. "Let your fountain be blessed, / and rejoice in the wife of your youth, / a lovely deer, a graceful doe. / Let her affection fill you at all times with delight, / be infatuated always with her love" (Proverbs 5:18–19).

Both husband and wife need to nurture affection, to delight in one another. They protect each other from temptation by meeting each other's needs for physical affection.

Our marriage is the core relationship of the family. Our spouse should be our primary priority, and our children second. We need to meet our children's needs without being consumed by them, with little left over for our spouse. By God's grace, we can maintain our priorities. Given the urgency of needs and the ages and number of your children, that may be easier said than done.

In particular, there is a legitimate and beautiful need for physical affection between spouses that nurtures their relationship and blesses all members of the family. Children enjoy seeing their parents smooch and snuggle—small acts of affection, not inappropriate intimacy. A Cincinnati couple I know refer to it as "snitchin' in the kitchen." Children walking in may groan, but the smiles on their faces belie their true feelings: Mom and Dad don't just love each other; they like each other!

When our small children would squeeze between us, I thought they were trying to separate us. Now I realize they just wanted to be included, to feel the crush of love.

Be on Guard

One of the ways Satan tries to destroy an effective witness is to destroy marriages. People involved in an apostolate—youth outreach, CCD, the diaconate, RCIA—need to be aware that they might be particular targets. Why? They are making inroads into the kingdom of darkness, and they may become vulnerable if they are not watchful.

Sometimes people get close spiritually—praying together or working in an apostolate together—and don't realize how vulnerable they are. They might not recognize as inappropriate small expressions of affection, gifts or personal sentiments. However, their positive responses to these small steps can lead to more of an entanglement. And that entanglement must be dealt with before it becomes a full-blown affair.

One time a pastor received a note from a parishioner that expressed inappropriate sentiments. He called her for an appointment and asked her to bring her husband. When they met, he asked her to read the letter aloud in her husband's hearing. After she did so, she asked both the pastor and her husband for forgiveness.

A woman approached Scott after one of his talks. She gave him a big hug that made him feel uncomfortable and then offered him a place to stay with her anytime he was speaking in the area. It may have been an innocent offer; however, Scott immediately said he didn't stay in women's homes on his trips. Then he alluded to me: Even the mention of a spouse's name can put a wet blanket on someone's smoldering temptation.

Some people, however, do not care if you and your husband are married. A wedding band just makes their ploy more of a challenge (and they might think there is less risk of venereal disease with a married person). And just because someone is "spiritual" does not mean she or he will not come after your spouse. You cannot afford to be naïve. "Be sober, be watchful. Your adversary the devil prowls around like a roaring lion, seeking some one to devour" (1 Peter 5:8).

Be wise in your friendships. Do not assume that just because someone is a good friend of the family, an affair could not happen. A good friend stops by occasionally, available when your spouse is not, and the next thing you know, your hearts can become entangled. That can lead to death: spiritual death and the death of your marriage.

Sometimes we can be particularly vulnerable when we have unresolved conflicts or disappointments in our marriage, such as financial stresses that our spouse will not shoulder. In loneliness and confusion we can reach out to someone who seems compassionate and share our hearts without considering what we have done: We have closed our heart to our spouse in some manner and opened it to another. This is especially dangerous if we are confident that nothing could tempt us to be unfaithful.

Marriage is the most intimate unveiling of one person to another. Treat such unveiling with reverence and awe. Guard the inner sanctum of your marriage. Do the work of the relationship with your spouse, listening to his heart and sharing your own, resolving conflicts and expressing tenderness and affection.

Getting Free

If we find ourselves becoming entangled with another person, what can we do?

First, pray for help and for wisdom. Saint James writes, "If any of you lacks wisdom, let him ask God, who gives to all men generously and without reproaching, and it will be given him" (James 1:5). God longs to give us wisdom.

Next, confess anything that is sinful, even if the actions are only imprudent decisions rather than deliberate sins. Flirtation, for example, can send a confusing message. It can be playful between two singles; once you marry, however, it can be dangerous. See it for what it is: not a compliment but an attack on your or the other person's marriage.

Finally, thank the Lord for your spouse. Set your heart on your beloved. This will help you to guard your marriage and build the foundation of faithfulness that warrants your husband's trust in you.

Chapter Six

How to Build Trust Daily

We build the foundation of trust through our thoughts, words and deeds. Here are some areas in which we can make daily progress in faithfulness toward our spouse.

Our Thoughts

Prayer First

Our prayer life is the cornerstone for building a foundation of trust. There are limits to what a husband or a wife can do; there are no limits to what God can do. In prayer we approach our heavenly Father as his beloved daughters and sons. We give him our praise for all he is doing, our concerns for all we face and for our loved ones, for whom he has greater love than we do. Each day we choose Christ in a kind of ongoing conversion. And each day we choose our spouses, praying for them.

The more we grow in grace, the more we yield to the Spirit's work in our life. The Spirit produces in us "love, joy, peace, patience, kindness, goodness, faithfulness, gentleness, self-control" (Galatians 5:22–23). Rather than tackling the challenges of married life with our own strength and abilities, we ask the Spirit to give us his strength. We pray for wisdom, knowing that the Lord takes delight in "a wife and husband who live in harmony" (Sirach 25:1).

We pray for purity, aware of temptation without being controlled by fear. Being on our guard is not the same as questioning the faithfulness of our spouses; suspicion and jealousy detract from our love. I anticipate faithfulness from me to Scott—and from Scott to me—but I also pray for faithfulness, watchful for temptations.

We also pray with *thanksgiving*. "Have no anxiety about anything, but in everything by prayer and supplication with thanksgiving let your requests be made known to God. And the peace of God, which passes all understanding, will keep your hearts and your minds in Christ Jesus" (Philippians 4:6–7). Anxiety accomplishes no good thing; prayer brings peace.

Purity of Thought

Never, ever entertain impure thoughts. Pornography tends to tempt men more than women, but lately, statistics reveal Internet porn sites drawing increasing numbers of women. Please do not discount this filth as innocuous or silly. It becomes a form of addiction with serious individual, familial and societal consequences.

Pornography is sad, degrading and humiliating; it destroys marriages and damages lives. Mental images from films, soap operas, racy novels, magazines or the

Internet are difficult to erase. Your spouse is the only man or woman you should see naked—the only one you should desire.

Lust begins in the mind, as Jesus preaches in the Sermon on the Mount: "You have heard that it was said, 'You shall not commit adultery.' But I say to you that every one who looks at a woman lustfully has already committed adultery with her in his heart" (Matthew 5:27–28).

Temptations are not sin; lingering on impure thoughts is. As soon as an impure thought comes, refuse it and replace it with a pure thought. Let your imagination honor the Lord and your spouse.

Saint Paul echoes the importance of godly thinking: "Finally, brethren, whatever is true, whatever is honorable, whatever is just, whatever is pure, whatever is lovely, whatever is gracious, if there is any excellence, if there is anything worthy of praise, think about these things" (Philippians 4:8).

Forgive From the Heart

We forgive as an act of the will. How forgiving we feel does not indicate whether or not we have forgiven the other.

Unlike God, we do not forget easily, even when we have forgiven truly. When we remember an incident, we should thank God that we have forgiven the people involved. (Mulling over past events, actions or words that we have already forgiven is actually sinful.)

Forgiveness from the heart helps us guard our marriage. "Hatred stirs up strife, / but love covers all offenses" (Proverbs 10:12).

A Thankful Spirit

Saint Paul emphasizes the importance of thankfulness: "Rejoice always, pray constantly, give thanks in all circumstances; for this is the will of God in Christ Jesus for you" (1 Thessalonians 5:16–18). God's will is for us to thank him always. We grow in faithfulness when we are cheerful and thankful, especially for our spouses.

We can accomplish many tasks—taking care of the house and the children—but if we have a sour attitude, if we allow bitterness to grow, if we do things in a perfunctory way, we deplete the joy inside of us and in our home. Conversely, when we do tasks with cheerfulness and thankfulness, we demonstrate trustworthiness.

When you are frustrated with how your spouse spoke or acted, consider the incident to be like a photo taken when he yawned. You would say, "The photo does not do him justice." Likewise, his poor behavior does not do him justice. Instead focus on a "transformation image" of your spouse: what is good, true and attractive about him. Recount to yourself and others the wonderful things he has said and done and the character qualities that drew you to him. And thank God for him.

Our Words

Pray Together

Pray as a couple and as a family. Blessed Mother Teresa liked to quote Father Patrick Peyton's line, "The family that prays together stays together." The closer a couple gets to God, the closer they draw to each other. This is the idea behind Archbishop Fulton Sheen's teaching that it takes three to get married.[1]

Prayer keeps suffering in perspective, whether it is suffering we experience together or suffering we inflict on each other. For love of the other, we imitate Christ's embrace of the cross: "For the joy that was set before him [he] endured the cross, despising the shame" (Hebrews 12:2). We focus on the joy of what God is accomplishing in and through us in the midst of suffering.

Speak the Truth in Love

Communicate respect at all times (see Ephesians 5:33), and expect respect from your spouse. You both want to share your thoughts and know they are valued. When you regularly communicate with respect, discussions about offenses, problems and difficulties are more fruitful. The goal is not to set each other straight or hurt each other but to speak the truth in love so that your relationship prospers.

For our family vacation one year, my dad selected this passage for us all to memorize: "Know this, my beloved brethren. Let every man be quick to hear, slow to speak, slow to anger, for the anger of man does not work the righteousness of God" (James 1:19–20). In other words, listen with true empathy. Too often we are quick to offer a solution rather than compassion. Respond rather than react to each other verbally, letting grace be the grease in the midst of possible friction. And in the midst of conflict, offer more light than heat by controlling anger. Choose peaceful resolutions to difficulties, as an angry outburst will only prolong efforts toward resolution.

We should work continually on communication skills in order to understand our differences. Words of affirmation should be many; words of criticism, few. We should develop rules about how to fight fair so as to minimize damage and maximize the resolution, always believing the best of the other. This is part of the lifelong process of caring for each other as beloved covenant partners.

Remember, God is more interested in making *you* holy than in using you to make your spouse holy. In humility let charity toward your spouse mature. Lead with love, as much as you can, before, during and after moments of conflict.

Raise concerns as gently as possible, speaking the truth in love. Keep in mind that timing is important. Remember that "faithful are the wounds of a friend" (Proverbs 27:6), and "a rebuke goes deeper into a man of understanding / than a hundred blows into a fool"

(Proverbs 17:10). If we grow together as men and women of understanding, we will build the foundation of trust and unconditional love that enables us to receive thoughtful rebukes and respond appropriately.

Communicate Clearly

Our communication skills improve when we grow in self-knowledge and a better understanding of our mate. There are a number of resources available to help us. The more we understand and appreciate the differences between us, the more patient we are with ourselves and with our spouses. Couples' retreats, such as Catholic Engaged Encounter and Worldwide Marriage Encounter, assist couples in good communication.[2]

Personality inventories, such as Myer-Briggs, help us pinpoint our natural strengths and weaknesses and understand sources of possible conflict. [3] For example, if one of us is an introvert and the other is an extrovert, we could have conflicts over how to spend social time. If we understand how each of us views things, we can adjust to the needs of the other, so that both of us feel we are taken seriously. Or if one is a planner and the other is more spontaneous, we can learn to appreciate the differences and find ways to share our strengths.

Temperament tests help us appreciate why we respond the ways we do.[4] They reveal virtues that are natural to us—we get less credit for having them than we first thought—and those that need more work because they are not natural. Increased understanding helps us to be more patient with ourselves and with others, all the while showing us areas that need work. The test results can also be useful in spiritual direction.

Another source of differences between spouses can be birth order.[5] Learning about this issue helped Scott and me understand a pattern in our conflict resolution. As a firstborn, I have a hard time apologizing first. Scott, a last born, apologizes easily. Why is that?

A firstborn is more experienced and more knowledgeable (at least for the first few years) than siblings. Being right a lot of the time does not lend itself to humility. A last born, on the other hand, tends to be wrong a lot of the time in relation to older siblings, which lends itself to humility. While this helps explain why Scott apologizes more easily than I do, it does not excuse me from growing in humility.

Another area of self-understanding that has blessed our marriage is the concept of love languages, as explained by Dr. Gary Chapman.[6] The five basic ways we express and interpret love include words of affirmation (genuine compliments, specific praise), gift giving (any kind of generosity—not materialistic), quality time (meaningful time together), physical touch and closeness (affection through hugs, kisses, wrestling, back rubs and so on) and acts of service (noticing and meeting needs without fanfare).

When we court we tend to express love in all of the languages; however, over time, we often revert to the love language that is most natural to us. When we neglect the love language of our spouse, he or she may feel less love from us. Small adjustments in our expressions of love can reopen communication and help us more effectively express love. "And over all these put on love, which binds everything together in perfect harmony" (Colossians 3:14).

I had just finished reading *The Five Love Languages* when a college co-ed called. She and her intended had called off their wedding, scheduled in six weeks. They knew they loved each other, but they no longer *felt* love for each other.

We met, and I explained the love languages to the young woman. I asked her if her love language might be "quality time." She said yes, and she was pretty sure that her ex-fiancé's was "words of affirmation." Then I asked her some critical questions: Was it possible that, in the midst of their extended engagement, they had neglected using each other's primary love language? Was he too busy working at a job and finishing school, so they could get married, to spend quality time with her? And when they actually had time together, was she critical of him rather than affirming? She looked at me in amazement. Yes, it was possible.

A week later the young woman tapped me on the shoulder at church and showed me her engagement ring! She had purchased Dr. Chapman's book, read it in a day and then passed it on to her ex-fiancé. It made sense to both: They *had* stopped speaking the primary love language of the other. When they took steps to change that, the wedding was back on. Two years later they are still glowing, grateful for the insight that helped restore their relationship.

We need to be multilingual in our love, using tender affection, kind words, gifts, acts of service and time spent well together. It is not enough to feel unconditional love for our spouse; we have to learn how we can communicate it so that our spouse feels it.

Never Lie

Never, ever, ever lie! "Lying lips are an abomination to the LORD, / but those who act faithfully are his delight" (Proverbs 12:22). Marriage is built on trust; even one lie puts a huge crack in its foundation. Your spouse counts on your telling the truth every time. Be faithful to your word, and expect the same from your beloved.

Single women, if you find out that a guy you are dating lies, you might want to walk away. Maybe you could rebuild that foundation, but maybe not.

Recently a woman called me and said, "I'm engaged to be married in three weeks, and I just found out today my husband-to-be was married before. He thought that since he had an annulment, he did not need to mention it. What should I do?"

I urged the woman to tell her fiancé right away that the wedding would not happen in three weeks. He had broken the foundation of trust in their relationship, and they needed time to see if that trust could be restored.

If you are already married when you discover your spouse lied to you, you both need to commit to rebuilding trust between you. It is an arduous task and will take time. Even with forgiveness, you will need to establish accountability. By God's grace, trust can be restored.

Practice Discretion

People who are close undoubtedly share personal things with each other. What do we do with the confidences shared with us? It is essential that we practice discretion and prudence when we share. As we grow in a friendship, and that friend sees us as faithful and able to keep confidences, friendship grows.

Likewise we honor the confidences, personal and professional, of our spouses. That includes not sharing our disagreements. "He who forgives an offense seeks love, / but he who repeats a matter alienates a friend" (Proverbs 17:9). Even sharing difficulties under the guise of prayer concerns can be gossip. "He who goes about as a talebearer reveals secrets, / but he who is trustworthy in spirit keeps a thing hidden" (Proverbs 11:13).

We need to guard our mouths. Saint Paul lists gossip among some very serious sins (see Romans

1:28–32). Whether or not it is based on truth, gossip is dangerous. Why? Because it harms people, harms unity and prohibits love from covering offenses.

Do not establish confidences apart from your spouse, either with your friends or your children. When someone asks me to keep something from Scott, I say that I have to be able to tell him. That does not mean I tell him everything—we hardly have time to talk about all the things we need to discuss, let alone share other people's situations. But our unity is too important to allow someone's confidence to keep us apart.

Children sometimes try the "divide and conquer" mentality. They will do something wrong and then beg me not to tell Dad. My response consistently is, "Honey, if you feel that I should not tell Dad, I must tell Dad. Dad needs to know, so that you have a good relationship." I cannot allow a child to become a wedge between us or maneuver me between his dad and him.

Some women are tempted to commiserate with their older daughters and sons about their husbands. Adults may not realize that they are breaking confidence with their spouse by establishing a deeper confidence with their children. Instead, we need to strengthen our children's relationships to our spouse by building bridges instead of walls.

Say the Words of Forgiveness

How truly do you forgive?

I tend to be a lawyer: I build a good case, list offenses and damages and excuse my misbehavior while I accuse another. Following the first major disagreement Scott and I had after our engagement, we met in the dorm lobby. I led the conversation.

"Scott, I was thinking about some things that are bothering me. So I wrote this little list. Number one,..." I read off each complaint. I wanted a clean slate.

Scott's response was brief: "Number one, I don't ever want to be greeted with a list again."

I got the point. Conflict resolution does not come from building a case against the other person.

One of the tricky things in marriage is knowing *when* to share your concerns as well as *how*. Something little goes wrong, and you think, *That's not a big deal; there's no need to even bring that up.* Then it happens the next day and the next. Now you see a pattern. What is your strategy?

Some people hold in their complaints and allow them to become deep sources of irritation. Can you imagine killing a spouse over squeezing the toothpaste tube in the middle or leaving hair in the sink one time too many? After thirty years Mary has had it, and Frank gets it! Granted, the response is rarely that desperate. Yet unresolved conflicts can allow anger, resentment and depression to rule a home instead of love.

It is important to find the balance between "offering up" the challenges and being honest about difficulties so that a relationship can flourish. All issues are not equal. We distinguish among flaws, weaknesses, irritations and sins.

Scott and I try to address concerns and forgive one another quickly. We call it "keeping short accounts"— dealing with small situations so they do not become big. "Above all hold unfailing your love for one another, since love covers a multitude of sins" (1 Peter 4:8).

Reminding your spouse of your forgiveness can become another criticism. If we want to be miserable, we can focus on how imperfect someone else is. Love chooses a better way: "Love bears all things, believes all things, hopes all things, endures all things" (1 Corinthians 13:7).

Contentment Versus Contentiousness

We constantly face a choice: Will we be content or contentious? Will we accept what we cannot change, or will we grumble and complain?

Both Proverbs 19:13 and 27:15 speak of a nagging wife as a constant drip. Proverbs 21:19 tells us, "It is better to live in a desert land / than with a contentious and fretful woman." Proverbs 21:9 and 25:24 both say, "It is better to live in a corner of the housetop / than in a house shared with a contentious woman." In the frustration of conflict, Scott has quoted this verse, half in jest and half seriously, while heading to his third-floor office.

Men also struggle against contentiousness in themselves. "As charcoal to hot embers and wood to fire, / so is a quarrelsome man for kindling strife" (Proverbs 26:21). Saint Paul urges a different attitude: "There is great gain in godliness with contentment; for we brought nothing into the world, and we cannot take anything out of the world" (1 Timothy 6:6–7). Contentment, not contentiousness, should be our response.

Our Deeds

Practice the Faith From a Sincere Heart

Take full advantage of the sacramental graces available to you, including frequent reception of the Eucharist and regular Confession. Keep the channels of grace unclogged, free from debris. Do not wait for a mortal sin before going to Confession: The path to mortal sin is beaten down through habits of venial sin. Be a maximalist rather than a minimalist.

Faithfulness to Christ includes faithfulness to his bride, the Church. We honor our spouse and his when we take to heart the Church's teaching on marriage. We need to learn the Church's teaching so that we can live it faithfully as a family.

Modest Dress

For whom are you dressing, your husband or someone else? Modest clothing is attractive rather than seductive. Clothing that draws attention to your face rather than other body parts honors your spouse, and he is the only one you should want to please.

A wife's charm delights her husband,
and her skill puts fat on his bones.
A sensible and silent wife is a gift of the Lord,
and there is nothing so precious as a disciplined
soul.
A modest wife adds charm to charm,
and no balance can weigh the value of a chaste
soul. (Sirach 26:13–15)

My mom prepared for my dad to come home from work. About fifteen minutes before he arrived, she put on fresh makeup and perfume, changed her outfit if it was dirty and brushed her teeth. She was ready to greet him.

I know that this is tough when you are making dinner and caring for little ones. However, welcoming your husband home sets the tone for dinner and the evening.

My dad's suggestion: Men, think of a place on the drive home where you set aside cares and focus on the joy awaiting you. Later you can share about what was tough about your day; now get ready to be welcomed home and to greet your family. Take time to appreciate the efforts your spouse has taken to prepare for you. A loving homecoming takes forethought.

Affection

Don't relegate the act of marriage to something perfunctory. Find the balance between "fast-food sex" and taking more leisure to enjoy intimacy.

Never withhold yourself from your spouse in order to manipulate or punish him. If you need more resolution in an argument before intimacy, be honest about that, but never refuse relations as a way of continuing the argument. In fact, sometimes a resolution to an argument is facilitated by intimacy, especially if the source of the tension is sexual frustration.

Saint Paul offers this warning:

> The husband should give to his wife her conjugal rights, and likewise the wife to her husband. For the wife does not rule over her own body, but the husband does; likewise the husband does not rule over his own body, but the wife does. Do not refuse one another except perhaps by agreement for a season, that you may devote yourselves to prayer; but then come together again, lest Satan tempt you through lack of self-control. (1 Corinthians 7:3–5)

Intimacy plays an important role in a marriage, even when a couple abstains for a prayerful concern.

Give Your Spouse No Cause for Suspicion

As I mentioned before, friendships with the opposite sex should only be developed with and through your spouse. If you have a close friend of the opposite sex before marriage, you have two choices that can strengthen your marriage: Look for ways you and your spouse can share that friendship as a couple, or pull back from that close friend. It takes real maturity to recognize that even a dear friend can become a stumbling block.

Avoid the appearance of evil. "Never dine with another man's wife, / nor revel with her at wine; / lest your heart turn aside to her, / and in blood you be plunged into destruction" (Sirach 9:9). In other words, avoid intimacy apart from your spouse.

If you receive compliments that meet a need that your spouse is failing to meet, work on your communication skills, and let your spouse know what more you need from him or her. Let the Lord use that occasion in your life to improve your marriage, rather than allow the attentions of others to become a wedge between you.

This applies in a similar way to spiritual attachments. Do not justify an illicit relationship on the premise that you are "soul mates." Your spouse is to be your soul mate. This is difficult if your spouse does not share the faith with you. If that is the case, pray and sacrifice for his or her conversion.

Keep the Marriage Bed Undefiled

Do not give Satan any foothold. Do not be naïve.

Following a talk in California, a wife asked me for advice. Her husband had purchased some porn films under the guise that it would help them improve their sex life. She wanted to know what I thought about it.

I told her, "There is nothing in those films you need to see to help you express marital love. He is becoming aroused by another woman and then using you to take care of that arousal. That is quasi-adultery. You must tell him you will never look at another porn film with him, and he must stop ordering them immediately. Any videos you currently have should be destroyed so that no children can find them in the trash.

> This material is destructive, not instructive, for marriages! It is an affront to your dignity as a woman and a defiling of your marriage bed. "Let marriage be held in honor among all, and let the marriage bed be undefiled; for God will judge the immoral and adulterous." (Hebrews 13:4)

Act With Integrity

The woman of faith acts in harmony with her husband's interests. In regard to finances, this includes creating and following a budget. What is essential—like food, clothing and shelter? What is desirable—like date nights, vacations and gifts?

Our experiences growing up may be very different. Some of us had parents who were spendthrifts, living on the edge of bounced checks and poor credit reports, purchasing items whimsically as long as the minimum could be paid monthly on the credit card bills. Others of us had parents who established budgets, lived within their means and planned for retirement. We need to talk about these variables and their influence on our present understanding of finances.

The woman of faith is frugal with money and possessions; that is one of the ways finances prosper in her hands. She follows the stewardship principle: If someone is faithful over a little, he or she will be given much (see Matthew 25:14–30).

Acting with integrity in terms of the family finances is a concrete way to express and to demonstrate trust in each other. Many decisions a couple makes in early marriage provide the financial foundation for greater peace and fewer conflicts for years to come.

We also want integrity to characterize our domestic duties. When we consistently do the things that we need to do, our families know they can depend on us. Mothers have trained some of us in this; others lack experience in this area. Through mentors—older or more accomplished women who can teach us—and through written materials, we can all develop better skills. In addition, we should desire to do even the smallest of tasks with great love.[7]

Deal With Temptations

Temptations are the gateway to sin, but they are not sinful themselves. Saint Paul assures us, "No temptation has overtaken you that is not common to man. God is faithful, and he will not let you be tempted beyond your strength, but with the temptation will also provide the way of escape, that you may be able to endure it" (1 Corinthians 10:13).

We are vulnerable to temptations, but we do not have to yield to them. We can appeal to Jesus as our sympathetic high priest, who was tempted in every way but did not sin (see Hebrews 2:14–18; 4:15). He understands our plight; therefore he has given us his Spirit—the Holy Spirit—to empower us to live the way he did.

To limit the power of temptation, we need to be honest about ways either of us feels vulnerable to adultery. This can include unmet needs in the areas of time together, help around the house or with the children, communication (lack of compassion, too much criticism, lack of compliments) or the need to make love more often.

Are You Caught in the Web of Adultery?

STOP! Now is the moment of grace. It is never too late for forgiveness and restoration. Get to Confession, both for forgiveness and for the grace to resist additional temptations. Accept God's forgiveness for you, and forgive yourself. Do not listen to the Accuser, who wants to keep you from the fullness of joy with your spouse.

Act decisively to avoid the near occasions of sin. Flee the fire of temptation. Cut off any relationship that has become an attachment. Remove yourself from situations that would place you with this other person; commit to total disengagement. Get out of the carpool, off the committee or out of the class. If you work with the person, do not go on that business trip together, and let your boss know you cannot travel alone with a member of the opposite sex. Find a new job if you need to.

Eliminate anything that could rekindle a flame in your heart for someone other than your spouse: photos, gifts, notes, e-mails and text messages. Do not return phone calls or reply to letters. Do not allow the other person an opportunity, however innocent, to downplay what you know in your heart is an attachment and to woo you back. This is not only about the survival of your marriage: Your very soul hangs in the balance, as does the soul of the person for whom you feel the attachment.

In committing adultery you have sinned not only against the Lord but also against your spouse. At the right time confess to your spouse, but do not give details that will make the deception even more painful.

There are no quick fixes: Broken trust has to be restored, and your spouse may need time before forgiveness replaces deep hurt. Build accountability. It may be helpful to have one trustworthy friend—a spiritual director, a priest or a family member—hold you accountable.

Break old habits and foster new ones. Fill your heart and mind with thankful thoughts about your spouse. Commit to memory certain Scriptures that address faithfulness.

Please consider a Retrouvaille Retreat with your spouse.[8] This is a retreat for couples who have serious problems in their marriages, such as adultery and alcohol or drug addiction. The retreat and a follow-up support group offer hope for restoration.

When it comes to fidelity in marriage, we need wisdom. If we act on the wisdom the Lord provides, we will strengthen our families; if not, we will weaken them. "Wisdom builds her house, / but folly with her own hands tears it down" (Proverbs 14:1). With wisdom the woman of faith fosters faithfulness so that the heart of her husband trusts in her.

Part Four

He Will Have No Lack of Gain
Proverbs 31:11b

CHAPTER SEVEN

Complementarity

The heart of her husband trusts in her, / and he will have no lack of gain" (Proverbs 31:11). The foundation of trust between a man and a woman is established through many opportunities to demonstrate integrity while courting. The couple then builds on this foundation through their covenant of marriage.

A Covenant Relationship

Many people approach marriage as a contract, but it is much more: It is a covenant. Contracts involve an exchange of goods and services. Covenants involve an exchange of persons: "I will be yours, and you will be mine."

Contracts are sealed with a promise by the two parties involved. Covenants are sealed with an oath: Two people call on God's name to seal the promise they have vowed before witnesses.

Contracts are limited: No ongoing relationship is necessary; only terms need be fulfilled. Covenants are perpetual, extending from generation to generation.

Contracts involve rights: Each party makes sure that his or her rights are respected. Covenants involve responsibilities: Each person gives himself or herself as a total gift to the other.

The covenant of marriage entails a sacrificial gift of one to the other. Like Christ, we are called to die to ourselves. Christ has withheld nothing from his bride, the Church, nor the Church from Christ. In imitation we withhold nothing from each other.

Jesus says, "If any man would come after me, let him deny himself and take up his cross and follow me. For whoever would save his life will lose it; and whoever loses his life for my sake and the gospel's will save it" (Mark 8:34–35). We find our life by offering it in service.

A contractual or conditional relationship is a contradiction to the cross. Prenuptial agreements reflect a contractual mind-set. Even before they marry, the couple agrees to the terms of a divorce. When the contract is broken, certain goods will go back to the original owner. This arrangement is based on distrust. It encourages the two persons to remain somewhat independent of each other.

One father told his daughter on her departure for her freshman year in college, "I want you to have this degree so that *when* you get divorced, you'll be able to support your children." Sadly, this father planted the seeds of distrust in his daughter's heart before she began to think seriously about marriage. Parents should play a critical role in helping their children understand the limitations of independence. Thankfully, others have planted seeds of hope in this young woman for a solid marriage where healthy interdependence anticipates faithful, fruitful, lifelong love. This is a covenantal approach to marriage.

Finances Flourish

The result of a husband's trust and a wife's trust-worthiness is that he has "no lack of gain." Our culture says that a husband has no lack of gain if his wife is earning a salary too: double income, no kids. Is this the meaning of the text?

No, this is not about a second wage earner in the family. The husband of the Proverbs 31 woman has no lack of gain, in part because his honest work increases under her supervision. The woman of faith helps care for the family's needs, all the while she is frugal. She does not spend money frivolously, nor is she stingy. She is generous to the poor and personally involved in works of charity (see Proverbs 31:20).

Through her assistance in managing family finances, she bolsters her husband's resolve to be faithful in his job, to never steal and to not cheat on taxes. He is not tempted to unjust gain, because he and his wife are satisfied with their financial situation.

Often people do not understand the actual cost of things, what economists refer to as *opportunity costs*. Spending less can mean more to the finances of the family than earning more, on which there are additional costs and taxes.

While I walked our firstborn, Michael, I ran into a neighbor who also had a new baby. Our conversation went like this:

"Oh, Mrs. Hahn, are you home full-time with your baby?"

"Yes," I said.

"Oh," she said, "that is the best. I had to fly my mother all the way over from Japan. I had to take her to English lessons and little craft lessons, so she wouldn't get bored. And we have to pay for her food. Oh, that is the best."

Then she asked, "Do you breast-feed?"

"Yes," I said.

"Oh, that is the best. We have to buy formula in those little cans. Then we have to sterilize the bottles and stick them in the fridge. Oh, that is the best."

Then she added, "Do you use cloth diapers?"

At this point I was feeling a bit embarrassed. "Yes," I said.

"Oh, that is the best. We have to buy the big boxes of Pampers with the little gathers, and oh, it's so expensive. It's a good thing I work; otherwise I could not afford all these things."

I did not know if I should laugh or cry. This new mom was gone long hours, making a two-hour commute every day into Washington, D.C., for a very high-pressure job. She did not intend to have another baby. Wasn't she even admitting it would be best to be home with this one who would be her only child?

Often many expenses are not factored into the equation of having a mom work outside of the home: new clothes, day-care or after-school baby-sitting, fast food and food expenses related to work, extra help with housework, transportation costs and even the extra taxes that come with a higher income bracket. A mom who is home full-time can save the family money, not to mention adding the peace factor of knowing children are well cared for—no nannycam needed.

There are other financial decisions prior to marriage that can add peace later. If you are unmarried, taking a semester to work in order to avoid deeper college debt might bless a future marriage more than graduating one semester earlier, though some college debt may fall into the category of capital debt. It is important to remember that "the rich rules over the poor, / and the borrower is the slave of the lender" (Proverbs 22:7). Debt is slavery, so do all you can to avoid it and to pay it down as quickly as possible.

If you are married and not yet blessed with children, establish a budget based on the husband's salary and save the wife's or apply it to debt reduction if you have any; this will ease the financial transition after children arrive. Debt "mortgages" the future and can make it very difficult to be open to life.

Did you know that a person cannot enter religious life as long as he or she has debt? That person's debt would be a burden to the diocese or the community. Why is this not just as true for the vocation of marriage?

It may seem preferable to own a home before you have a baby, but little ones can live quite well in a rental unit. And when you do go to buy a home, avoid any that would stress the budget so much that you cannot be open to life. You do not have to move into the kind of home that your parents now own. Nor do you need new furniture or a new car for status. Good financial decisions will bless your marriage.

Generosity

The prophet Malachi admonishes Israel to take the Lord seriously about tithing:

> Will man rob God? Yet you are robbing me. But you say, "How are we robbing you?" In your tithes and offerings. You are cursed with a curse, for you are robbing me; the whole nation of you. Bring the full tithes into the storehouse, that there may be food in my house; and thereby put me to the test, says the LORD of hosts, if I will not open the windows of heaven for you and pour down for you an overflowing blessing. (Malachi 3:8–10)

The blessing God promises is not the stuff of televangelists, who exhort people to give so that they will be healthy and wealthy. It is the blessing of obedience.

The tithe is 10 percent of earnings (not gifts) before taxes: We give God, not the government, the first 10 percent. There are two ways to look at this. Either we *have* to give God 10 percent and make our budget work with less. Or God owns 100 percent and *lets* us keep 90 percent for our family's needs. One perspective makes us feel as if God is miserly; the other focuses on God's generosity. He lets us use our resources to build the kingdom while we care for our family.

Scott and I have always honored the principle of the tithe, even when he was in graduate school. The year we made less than ten thousand dollars, by the grace of God we still gave 10 percent off the top. At first I looked at the checks I was writing and almost gasped. "Lord, how can I give fifty dollars to anything? We need this money!" But I believed that we needed to be obedient, so I wrote the checks.

Then I realized that we were never going to be too poor to give to God; 10 percent of something small is *still* something. Remember the widow's sacrificial giving of her two coins? It was not the amount as much as the sacrifice that pleased our Lord. Though Scott and I were poor, the Lord always provided what we needed. We learned, over and over, that we couldn't outgive God, for he will not be outdone in generosity.

Do not make excuses: I will tithe when I am no longer a student, or after I pay off my credit cards, or once I get the down payment for a house.... To delay obedience is disobedience, just as we tell our children. Establish the habit of tithing now. It will never be easier than it is today, and there always will be excuses to wait.

We train our children that when they earn a dime, they give a penny to the Lord. When they earn a dollar, they bring him ten cents. Recently my son realized where this was going. "When I make a thousand dollars, am I going to have to give a hundred?"

I smiled. "That's right, honey, you *get* to give a hundred." It never gets easier, but the habit makes it possible and prepares us to have joy in it.

> The point is this: he who sows sparingly will also reap sparingly, and he who sows bountifully will also reap bountifully. Each one must do as he has made up his mind, not reluctantly or under compulsion, for God loves a cheerful giver. And God is able to provide you with every blessing in abundance, so that you may always have enough of everything and may provide in abundance for every good work. (2 Corinthians 9:6–8)

Numerous proverbs refer to the stewardship of resources: If we are faithful over a little, then God will give us more resources to manage. In addition to tithing (yes, there's more), Jesus refers to almsgiving, assuming we will give beyond the tithe. He says, "But *when* you give alms, do not let your left hand know what your right hand is doing, so that your alms may be in secret; and your Father who sees in secret will reward you" (Matthew 6:3–4, italics mine). Tithing is the beginning of Christian giving, and our hope is that we can be generous financially beyond the ten percent required.

Studies place the average giving of American Catholics between 0.5 and 1.5 percent! Imagine what our country would be like, what we could do as the Church, if Catholics tithed? We have been called to sacrificial giving both to express our gratitude for how blessed we are and to care for the poor in Jesus' name.

Strategy for Finances

Husband and wife make wise financial decisions jointly. He brings home the bread; it is not *his* paycheck but the *family* paycheck. She multiplies it through good stewardship. Together husband and wife establish a budget and follow it; hopefully this is a skill both bring to marriage. There is a sense of teamwork instead of the frustration of pulling away from each other.

Financial difficulty is a main cause of marital stress. In fact, money troubles are the number one reason given for divorce. So this is an important area in which a couple should take advantage of whatever practical help they can get from parents, respected older adults and available materials on money management. A couple's prayerful and respectful reflections help them develop a financial strategy for short-term and long-term goals. This process strengthens their relationship and contributes to the peace of their home.

A simple strategy is to set aside 10 percent of the gross for a tithe and 10 percent of the net for savings, and then budget the rest according to needs. Some people use the envelope system: They put cash in envelopes designated for food, clothing, entertainment and so forth, and when the month's money for a particular category is gone, it is gone.

When you first establish a budget, you may not know how much is needed for particular items, such as food and gas. You may need to revise the budget monthly until you get it right.

Complementary Service

This gets us back to the issue of trust. The wife trusts that her husband is serving the family through his work instead of pursuing his own interests while she is stuck at home. The husband trusts that his wife is serving the family through her work in the home instead of resenting her for having fun with the children or not "carrying her load" of the finances. When trust is the foundation of the relationship, the service of husband and wife strengthens the other, and the couple find joy in the complementarity of their service to the family.

When people ask me, "Do you work?" I'm really stumped. I hate saying no: I work seven days a week, twenty-four hours a day. A note on my fridge says, "Do I work? Of course I work! I'm a mother!" There's no pay, but the benefits are out of this world! Vacations are usually on the job.

When one of Scott's students asked if I worked, he responded, "Yes, she's home full-time."

The student, thinking Scott did not understand the question, asked, "No, I mean, does she work?"

Knowing exactly what the student was asking, Scott responded, "Yes, she's home full-time."

A slightly frustrated freshman posed the question one more time. "Does your wife have a job outside the home?"

To which Scott said, "You mean, is she a part-time mother? No, she's home full-time."

Of course, one of the hardships in being a mom who works outside the home is that you are still a full-time mom. So even when you are not with your children, you are concerned for their well-being. You carry the weight of mothering into your job, and this is a lot to bear.

Both spouses serve the Lord and the family. We do not ignore our personal interests or needs, but we place others' interests before our own.

> So if there is any encouragement in Christ, any incentive of love, any participation in the Spirit, any affection and sympathy, complete my joy by being of the same mind, having the same love, being in full accord and of one mind. Do nothing from selfishness or conceit, but in humility count others better than yourselves. Let

each of you look not only to his own interests, but also to the interests of others. (Philippians 2:1–4)

Family Flourishes

God—the Father, Son and Holy Spirit—is a communion of interpersonal, life-giving love. God creates man and woman in his image to reflect this self-sacrificing love, and he places them in a marital relationship.

> Then God said, "Let us make man in our image, after our likeness."...So God created man...; male and female he created them. And God blessed them, and God said to them, "Be fruitful and multiply, and fill the earth and subdue it; and have dominion over the fish of the sea and over the birds of the air and over every living creature that moves upon the earth." (Genesis 1:26–28)

God's first command to man and woman is both a blessing and a command. They are to be fruitful, to bear children as life-giving lovers. Their children embody the unity of husband and wife. They reveal the life-giving power of love.

Yet there are couples who choose to be childless. They promote the idea of an exclusive focus on each other, unhampered by little ones. In a "Cathy" cartoon one character asks, "Aren't you worried about running out of time to have a baby, Cathy?" After a few comments Cathy poignantly concludes, "I'm torn between wanting to have one and wanting to be one." Sadly, this may sum up the inner conflict of a number of young adults.

Rather than seeing children in negative terms—depleting our resources, taking up space in our homes and infringing on our time—we need to see them the way God sees them. "Indeed children are the supreme gift of marriage and greatly contribute to the good of the parents" (*Gaudium et Spes*, 50).

Openness to new life is an integral part of our witness to the world about how our relationship reflects the relationship between Christ and the Church. The purpose of marriage is "to show forth to all men Christ's living presence in the world and the authentic nature of the Church by the love and generous fruitfulness of the spouses, by their unity and fidelity, and by the loving way in which all members of the family cooperate with each other" (*Gaudium et Spes*, 48). Generosity within the family, exemplified by fruitfulness, deepens the love of each family member for the others and bolsters the witness of the couple in the world.

Even a woman's body reveals her unique place in the lives of her children. Her body nurtures the life within her and then sustains that life through her milk. Her curved hips make it easier to balance a baby while doing other work, and extra fat on her arms helps her naturally to cradle a baby. God designed a woman's body this way.

Yet what are the messages bombarding young women today about their bodies and their ability to nurture life? Ultrathin models parade on runways. TV ads for the pill and the mini-pill feature beautiful couples dancing, walking and laughing while a narrator lists the possible side effects: heart attack, stroke and blood clots, just to name a few! Recent ads encourage young women to cope with their fertility by limiting it or even eliminating it. Coaches encourage women to exercise to such an extent that their periods stop, making it easier for them to compete.

There are subtler messages young women receive relative to career and education. A woman who would like to be a lawyer or a doctor receives the response, "That's impressive." If she wants to be in politics or even run for a top office, the response might be, "You are ambitious; good for you!" But if she says she wants to be a wife and a mom, the response is frequently, "Isn't that a waste of your education, your opportunities, your talents and your brains?" What television shows or movies, set in modern times, depict women who are bright, attractive and talented homemakers, with hearts and arms open to embrace a large family?

I did not expect this bias from friends. I took Michael, my ten-month-old firstborn, to the homecoming game at Grove City College, my alma mater. A former classmate saw us and asked, in all seriousness, "Are you taking a class? How are you using your brain?"

How was I using my brain? I was incredulous. What a limited perspective!

I paused to collect myself. "To be honest, nothing has demanded more of me physically, emotionally, mentally, intellectually or spiritually than having this little boy and wanting to share all of life with him."

The Ministry of Presence

Our culture promotes the idea that power is outside of the home in the workplace: If you want power, you need a position and a paycheck. The more power a woman wants, the more she needs to be a part of the workforce. A woman at home relinquishes power. She needs to be liberated from menial work that "anyone can do" in order to "earn her share."

God calls the woman of faith to be more than a supermom who juggles kids, housework and work outside the home; he calls her to be a dominion woman. She reigns in her home as queen, vice regent over her household. This is a noble position. She does not need power; she has authority. This reminds me of a conversation a friend overheard.

A couple of children were playing "ship" next door. The little boy declared, "I'm going to be the captain!"

The little girl retorted, "No, I'm going to be the captain!"

They argued back and forth. Then, after a dramatic pause, the girl said, "OK, you can be the captain. I'll be the captain's mother!"

The little boy's triumphant smile faded. "No, you won't!" he protested. Why? He knew what we know: She who rocks the cradle rules the world. The captain had power, but his mother had authority over him.

The question for us is not "How can I have power?" but rather "How can I serve?" God calls both husband and wife to serve him for the sake of the family, but the service looks different for each of them. As Pope John Paul II said, "To serve...means to reign."[1]

Providing for the family is the responsibility of the husband, as I mentioned in chapter three (see 1 Timothy 5:8). The marketplace is his primary sphere of service to the family. For those of us called to the vocation of wife and mother, our primary sphere of service is our home. In the give-and-take of external and internal service, we find the complementarity of the sexes.

A wife's contribution is real even if it is not always as tangible as a man's paycheck. She contributes much more than a paycheck: a stable presence, a ground of being for all of the members of the family. Children do not need caregivers, super-special day-care centers or after-school programs. They need their mom.

One mom who decided to quit work and come back home full-time found out that no other mother on her cul-de-sac was home in the afternoons. Quickly she came to know a number of neighbor children. One day a neighbor's daughter, Susie, burst through this mom's kitchen door, grinning from ear to ear. She had just made the cheerleading squad.

The woman reveled in Susie's accomplishment. "Show me your winning cheer, and then we'll celebrate with some cookies I just made!"

The next day the woman saw Susie's mother and asked her what she thought of her daughter's making the squad. Surprised, the mother said, "Susie didn't mention it when I came home from work last night." This mom missed the moment.

Transformed Thinking

"Do not be conformed to this world but be transformed by the renewal of your mind, that you may prove what is the will of God, what is good and acceptable and perfect" (Romans 12:2). Our minds have to be renewed so that we know the difference between what the world expects of us and what the Lord wants of us. This includes a frank discussion about what the Church teaches versus what the world presumes. Here are some primary examples.

First, the Church teaches that, as a rational act of obedience, each act of marriage should be open to life. The world assumes that, if a woman is a thinking person, she will use contraception. If that fails (that is, she gets pregnant), she will choose abortion or at least be sterilized to make contraception permanent for the future.

Second, the Church teaches that marriage is an indissoluble bond: It cannot be broken. The world assumes that marriage is not needed if two people love each other. Further, two people who do marry should be free to end that arrangement and move on to other people.

Third, the Church teaches that a couple should refrain from doing married things until they are married. In particular, cohabitation is not a trial marriage that will bless the relationship. The world says it is common sense to live together as a couple before marriage to find out about compatibility and to save money. If it does not work, then the couple can part ways without an expensive and nasty divorce.

However, cohabiting is much more dangerous than "playing house." It is trying to live married life without the sacramental graces necessary for it to succeed. In fact, both the man and the woman thwart the graces of Confession and the Eucharist if they are still receiving these sacraments, searing their consciences and hardening their hearts.

No one enters an intimate relationship planning for it to fail; however, cutting off graces needed to succeed will insure its failure. Jesus said. "I am the vine, you are the branches. He who abides in me, and I in him, he it is that bears much fruit, for apart from me you can do nothing" (John 15:5). As long as we remain connected to Jesus, we will bear good fruit. In the covenant of marriage, we will be blessed with faithful and fruitful love, and in turn we will be a blessing to our children and others around us.

We need to understand what the Church teaches and why. Unlike other denominations of Christians, who have a smorgasbord of theological and ethical choices before them, the Church has given us a unified moral teaching to understand and embrace. We cannot pick and choose what we will believe and how we will live. A woman handed me a note after a presentation: "I had an appointment for my sterilization next week. I'm going to cancel it: The cafeteria is closed!"

We need to understand the truth, so that our obedience is not perfunctory but rooted in our hearts. Jesus said, "If you continue in my word, you are truly my disciples, and you will know the truth, and the truth will make you free" (John 8:31–32). The Catholic Church proclaims the truth she has received, believes and lives. We are to follow her example. Thus the Lord frees us to love and serve him in ways that please him.

Queen of the Realm, Heart of the Home

In imitation of the queen mother in Proverbs 31, the woman of faith sees herself as the queen who reigns beside her beloved. The king rules, but the queen has real authority as well. She exercises dominion in the realm in which God has placed her as she nurtures her family.

What a contrast to the feelings of several college women who shared with me privately in my home. They struggled with very negative images of being at home full-time once they have children. Each woman used a different image: a doghouse where she is chained, a cage where she is enclosed, a jail. These are heartbreaking images that must be replaced with the beautiful images of what is possible.

Home should not be an unwelcome place from which a woman needs to be liberated so that she can be herself. Instead, home should be the place where each member of the family is loved unconditionally and feels safe and secure. Home is to be a haven of love and healing and warmth.

Home is the province of the woman of faith. It is a sanctuary, a place where she welcomes weary ones. With her skills, abilities, talents and sensitivities, she creates an environment in which every family member can thrive. She brings order and beauty to her home. She is in the heart of the home as the heart of the family.

God calls a wife to be her husband's helper, uniquely fit to assist him in particular. Sometimes that means delaying dreams to enable her spouse to pursue his. For example, my mom is a talented singer and an excellent teacher, and she generously offers her talents at church. However, when we were young and life was hectic with all that my father as pastor needed to do at church, she taught us and sang to us at home. She knew that if she were busy at church, we could resent both our parents for putting church activities first. I never heard her complain about not being able to use her talents publicly when we were young. She played her supporting role very well and still does.

The adage "Behind every great man is a great woman" is true. In fact, a man cannot be great if his wife views her role competitively. However, if she sees her challenge as helping her husband accomplish what dreams God has for him, she will be deeply satisfied in their complementarity, and both she and her husband "will have no lack of gain."

CHAPTER EIGHT

Healthy Interdependence

God is the one who created man and woman and established them in marriage, and he providentially oversees all families. Saint Paul said, "I bow my knees before the Father, from whom every family in heaven and on earth is named" (Ephesians 3:14–15). God is intimately involved in building our marriages and families into a civilization of love.

Vatican II told us, "For the good of the partners, of the children, and of society this sacred bond no longer depends on human decision alone. For God himself is the author of marriage.... The intimate union of marriage, as a mutual giving of two persons, and the good of the children demand total fidelity from the spouses and require an unbreakable unity between them" (*Gaudium et Spes*, 48).

In marriage a man and a woman flourish in an interpersonal communion of love. They function within the order of authority and the order of love in their marriage. This contributes to their children's well-being and the common good of society.

The Order of Authority

Adam is head of the first family *before* the fall from grace. Adam is created first. He names all of the animals, exercising his dominion over creation. When God presents Eve to Adam, Adam also names her and welcomes her as his chosen helper. The order of authority in the home is not the result of sin; the struggle between man and woman relative to authority is.

The Lord prophesies the consequences of Adam and Eve's sin, including disharmony between them in the area of authority: "To the woman he said, / 'I will greatly multiply your pain in childbearing; / in pain you shall bring forth children, / *yet your desire shall be for your husband, / and he shall rule over you'*" (Genesis 3:16, emphasis mine). She will desire to dominate him, but he will rule her. This vying for the dominant position in the family is a consequence of sin, not the solution to it. The solution to it is the order of authority, rooted in the mystery of authority in the Godhead.

The Father has revealed an order of authority within the Trinity: The Father sends the Son (see John 4:34), and the Father and the Son send the Holy Spirit (John 15:26). Yet each Person in the Godhead is fully God. There is functional subordination without any diminishing of the nature or the importance of any of the three Persons.

Likewise in marriage, there is an order of authority within the home: The husband is the head of the wife, and the husband and the wife together have authority over their children. That does not mean that a husband is smarter, more spiritual or morally better than his wife. Both husband and wife are made equally in the image and likeness of God (see Genesis 1:26–27), are equally in need of salvation (Genesis 3:22–23) and are equally saved by Christ (Galatians 3:28), as stated previously. Yet the wife is subordinate to the husband in the order of authority (see Ephesians 5:22 below). Just as in the Trinity, there is functional subordination in marriage without any diminishing of the nature or the importance of any person.

All authority has been given to Christ; so human authority is derivative. It is essential that a husband see himself, not just his wife, as being under authority. Both husband and wife, out of reverence for Christ, submit to him.

> Be subject to one another out of reverence for Christ. Wives, be subject to your husbands, as to the Lord. For the husband is the head of the wife as Christ is the head of the Church, his body, and is himself its Savior. As the Church is subject to Christ, so let wives also be subject in everything to their husbands. Husbands, love your wives, as Christ loved the Church and gave himself up for her, that he might sanctify her, having cleansed her by the washing of water with the word, that he might present the Church to himself in splendor, without spot or wrinkle or any such thing, that she might be holy and without blemish. Even so husbands should love their wives as their own bodies. He who

> loves his wife loves himself....Let each one of you love his wife as himself, and let the wife see that she respects her husband. (Ephesians 5:21–28, 33)

This is a recommended reading for the Rite for Celebrating Marriage During Mass.[1]

Strengthened Through Service

Some Scripture scholars misconstrue the Greek words in Ephesians 5:21 to mean that husbands and wives should be submissive to each other, contravening any order of authority within the home. The text does not support this. There certainly is a call to be deferential to and loving and respectful of each other (*CCC*, 1642); however, there is clearly an order of authority within marriage—based on the order of authority between Christ and the Church—taught in this passage. Christ is not just as submissive to the Church as the Church is to Christ.

The husband's authority is derived from God, and he is called to lead his marriage and his family. His wife's authority is derived from the Lord *and* from her husband: She is to submit to him in everything and to assist him in leading the family. The children have their own measure of authority, depending on birth order, and they are to submit to their father and their mother in everything. The context for all authority within the family is service to the Lord and each other. It is having dominion, not domination.

The model for men is Christ's servant leadership, which demonstrates his love for his spouse, the Church. This kind of sacrificial leadership is the opposite of dominating, abusive power exerted over a wife. As Jesus said, "The Son of man came not to be served but to serve, and to give his life as a ransom for many" (Matthew 20:28).

The husband's job includes spiritual leadership. He is responsible to present his wife as pure and without blemish to the Father, just as Christ presents the Church pure and spotless to his heavenly Father. The husband must know the Word of God well enough to cleanse his wife with the Word.

The model for women is the Church in her response of love and respect for Christ's leadership. It may seem difficult to us women to submit to a fallible man—as opposed to the Church's submission to the infallible God-man. Yet the husband's call is the more difficult one. The Lord will judge us on the basis of our response to our husbands; he will judge our husbands on the basis of how Christlike their leadership has been.

Too often Christians recoil from the notion of an order of authority in the home because they have seen this abused. However, the abuse is what should be jettisoned rather than the order of authority. When a couple respects the order of authority and the order of love in their home, peace prevails.

During the first year of our marriage, we attended

three weddings. The ceremonies were beautiful, the Scripture readings were inspiring, the music was uplifting, and we were deeply grateful for each other—at least, until after the ceremony.

Typically one of the readings would touch on the order of authority in the home. Our conversation on the way to the reception began in one of two ways. Either Scott said to me, "If you would submit more quickly to me or show me more respect, it would be so much easier to serve you and love you." Or I would say, "Scott, if you would love me more sacrificially, like Christ, it would be so much easier to be respectful and to follow your leadership."

In either case the simple suggestion, spoken with gentleness at first, quickly became an accusation. We would get so upset that we could barely go into the receptions happy with each other.

The third time this happened, we caught the pattern. We agreed that our inversion of Saint Paul's words were part of the problem. He does not say, "Wives, make sure your husbands love you sacrificially like Christ; husbands, make sure your wives submit to you in everything." Instead he says, "Let each one of you love his wife as himself, and let the wife see that she respects her husband" (Ephesians 5:33). If Scott and I would focus on our part, we would make it that much easier for the other to do his or her part. After all, our part was the part we could change.

This was a more helpful focus than trying to work on the other person to get him or her to change.

Marriage is work, involving conflict resolution: You choose either to pull together or pull apart, to protect yourself or to protect your bond of love by extending trust and sacrificial love. Men are commanded to love their wives, to nourish and cherish them as they would their own bodies; women are commanded to respect their husbands. It seems it would be easier for men to be irresponsible and lazy, relinquishing leadership to their wives, who want to run things. It would be easier for women to be willful and take charge. But what is easier is not what is best.

Ultimately neither men nor women are happy when God's authority within the home is subverted. Instead we need to do what is more difficult: Men, become loving servant leaders of your wives; women, show your husbands respect. This is one of the primary ways a marriage witnesses to the world the relationship between Christ and the Church.

Submission Strengthens Servant Leadership

Wifely submission is active obedience; it is not passivity. A wife's submission is rooted in her love and submission to the Lord first and to her husband second. (Obviously, if a husband should require disobedience to Christ, a wife should not comply.) This is service, not servitude.

A wife's submission to her husband strengthens his ability to lead. She cannot wait until she thinks he is worthy of such respect or trust before she follows him. She responds to his leadership in ordinary concerns and spiritual matters. Her response calls forth his responsibility before God. The respect she shows her husband sets the tone of respect in the home; the children will follow her example.

Jesus contrasts his style of leadership with that of the Gentiles, who "lord it over" others (see Matthew 20:25–27). The husband is to be a servant leader like Jesus in the home. His leadership provides a protection, a covering, a sense of security for his wife and children.

What about submission to a man who is not a Christian? If this is your situation, remember that your husband is still your husband. Scripture has advice for you too: "Likewise you wives, be submissive to your husbands, so that some, though they do not obey the word, may be won without a word by the behavior of their wives, when they see your reverent and chaste behavior" (1 Peter 3:1–2).

Though the *Catechism* does not explicitly address a wife's honorable obedience, it does refer to the "rights and duties in the Church between spouses" (*CCC*, 1631). In his encyclical *On Christian Marriage*, Pope Leo XIII refers to Ephesians 5:21–23 in the context of marital rights and duties:

The mutual duties of husband and wife have been defined, and their several rights accurately established. They are bound, namely, to have such feelings for one another as to cherish always a very great mutual love, to be ever faithful to their marriage vow, and to give one another an unfailing and unselfish help. The husband is the chief of the family and the head of the wife.[2]

We need to read Ephesians 5. Remember what Jesus said about knowing the truth and the truth setting us free (see John 8:32). Properly understood and lived, our marriages will be on more solid footing if we follow Scripture's teaching rather than current cultural dictates.

A Husband Worthy of Trust

What kind of leadership does Jesus Christ offer? First, he is unequivocally the King of Kings. No one wonders who leads the Church. Yet he leads by laying down his life for his bride. What does he hold back from the Church? Absolutely nothing. He gives the Church his life, his Body, his Blood, his soul, his divinity.

Likewise a husband is to hold back nothing from his spouse. God calls him to love his wife and lead her spiritually. He is to know the Word of God. It is his responsibility to present his wife holy to the Lord.

Hopefully you have selected a spouse who values your thoughts, who desires your wisdom and who cares about your feelings. Together you work on good communication skills. You have harmonious goals toward which you are working. Yet there can be situations in which you do not experience a meeting of the minds. Then the husband needs to lead his family in the direction he believes to be best. He should be able to expect his wife to follow his lead with a good attitude, even when she disagrees with his decision.

It is essential that we understand God's plan for the order of authority within the home. This is an integral part of the vows that we make on our wedding day.

Order of Love

Pope John Paul II emphasized another order that functions within marriage, the order of love. Just as the husband is the head of the home, so his wife is the heart of the home. He is first in the order of authority, and she is first in the order of love.[3]

There is something special within a woman that tunes in to love within the family, and her husband needs to welcome her thoughts and intuitions in order to foster this love. A wise man listens to the heart of his beloved.

When we speak of the order of authority in the home, we do not imply that the man is more important than the woman. Likewise, in the order of love, the woman is not more important than the man. The emphasis is on service for the good of the entire family.

The woman of faith is perceptive about her husband's needs: She knows them and meets them. She knows what is needed for good health, and she cares for him when he is sick. She brings honor rather than shame to his name. She builds up the family by bearing children, nurturing them and teaching them. And their estate prospers in her hands. She leads with love.

Which is more important, the head of the home or the heart of the home? Or which can you live without? The truth is that both are essential for a happy, healthy and holy marriage and family. The goal is for both husband and wife to be deferential in the interest of harmony and faithful to their specific roles as head and heart of the home.

This is a beautiful vision—and its accomplishment a daunting task—for both the husband and the wife. It takes a lot of trust to develop this kind of healthy interdependence. Both spouses need to call upon the grace of God to fulfill their roles in a way pleasing to him, all the while remembering Saint Paul's words, "I can do all things in him who strengthens me" (Philippians 4:13).

PART FIVE

She Does Him Good, and Not Harm

Proverbs 31:12a

CHAPTER NINE

Embracing Commitment

When a man and a woman discern the vocation of marriage, they move from a private promise to each other—I am my beloved's, and he is mine—to a public engagement. They approach the Church, at least six months before their hoped-for wedding date, to formalize their commitment. They prepare by learning more about what the Church teaches regarding marriage, for "marriage introduces one into an ecclesial *order*, and creates rights and duties in the Church between the spouses and towards their children" (*CCC*, 1631). When they marry they do not simply become a churchgoing couple but are an integral part of the mission of the Church based on their sacramental union.

When bride and groom state their vows as freely consenting adults, they confer the sacrament of Matrimony on each other (see *CCC*, 1623). They consent to live their vocation in conformity to the Church's teaching, and the priest receives their consent and blesses them on behalf of the Church. This is more than a special blessing: It is nothing less than the epiclesis of the Holy Spirit, which bride and groom receive "as the communion of love of Christ and the Church" (CCC, 1624).

It is most fitting for the couple to say their vows in the midst of the Mass, celebrating both sacraments of union and Communion. Mass is the life-giving sacrifice of the Bridegroom for his bride, the Church, to strengthen her faithfulness and fruitfulness. Likewise, the newly married couple pledge themselves to each other in faithfulness and fruitfulness. They approach the inner sanctum of the marriage bed, ready to receive the gift of the other in joy and purity and to receive children, should God bless their union with new life. This is their covenant renewal of union and communion, which strengthens their faithfulness and fruitfulness.

Embracing the commitment of marriage entails embracing God's design for the act of marriage. Committed men and women know the value and joy of that act. They give themselves solely to their spouses and thereby experience God's beautiful design for sexual intercourse: It strengthens their bond of love, gives deeply peaceful and joyful expression to their love and makes them cooperators with God in the creation of new life.

If you talked about consecrated wine, you would not describe it as really good wine. Even if you said it was great wine, you would miss the mark. Why? Because consecrated wine is holy, consecrated for sacred use. Similarly, the marriage act reveals that our bodies are consecrated for sacred use. The husband as priest of the home is received into the temple of his wife's body; they reflect the unity conferred on them through the sacrament. This is why the act of marriage is saved for marriage: It is holy.

In the committed relationship of marriage, the act of marriage bonds and blesses husband and wife.

In Joy and in Sorrow

Let's examine the vows a couple make. Pronounced for the most part in the flower of youth, are they rash vows? No. However, a couple rarely know fully at the time of their wedding what their vows entail. And given the realities of life, maybe that's a good thing.

"Rejoice with those who rejoice, weep with those who weep" (Romans 12:15). In marriage we practice the art of coming alongside the other, being a comforter, like the Holy Spirit. Whether we had a great day or not, we welcome our spouse home, ready to listen with compassion to the joys and sorrows of the day. We try to lift our spouse's spirits through encouragement, more than solve problems.

We also share our day. We allow one another to share dreams, and we do not belittle them. Our discussions include reality checks on what is possible. We look for joy in the life we share and avoid negative humor.

Saint Paul admonishes us, "Bear one another's burdens, and so fulfil the law of Christ" (Galatians 6:2).

This is how we love one another: We bear all things through genuinely caring for each other.

One of the difficulties moms with small children face is that, by the end of the day, they have been touched and touched. A woman may feel that she really does not want any more physical affection that day. Yet her spouse has not been touched all day. She needs to be responsive to him, especially if touch is his primary love language.

If this is your situation, you might ask for a few minutes to regroup, once the little ones are in bed, before you can be available physically to your spouse. It would be much better to ask your husband for some time to prepare than to decline his invitation to intimacy.

The same can be true for conversation. Even though many women tend to talk more than men, if your children have talked to you from morning till night, you may crave some silence.

My children were great conversationalists from early on, saying wonderful and cute things. By day's end I had listened a lot. Scott would ask, "Do you want to listen to a tape? Or do you want me to put on some music? Do you want to talk?"

My response was, "No, I just want to sit on the sofa for about fifteen minutes and be quiet, with no one touching me and no one talking to me." After I drank in the silence, I would find Scott in his study and enjoy our conversation. If the need for listening was urgent, however, I relinquished my "right" to do things the way I wanted and instead focused on serving my beloved.

This is the call to follow Christ: to serve rather than to be served. It means affirming your spouse, even when you feel unappreciated. It means asking him what you can do for him, expressing the love languages of gift giving or acts of service, even though you are tired from serving your children all day.

The phrase "in joy and in sorrow" seems particularly apropos in relation to receiving children. Is there a joy to compare with the discovery that a baby is on the way or, even more, safely delivered? Each child intensifies and enriches your love for your spouse. On the other hand, what great grief we experience in struggles with infertility or the death of a child.

When Scott and I lost babies in miscarriage, we did not grieve the same way. It was not essential that we felt or expressed grief the same way but that we shared with one another our sense of loss. We believed the other person felt loss and trusted each other to offer strength through the shared sorrow.

Sometimes parents offer their adult children false solutions to their suffering. They may withhold the Church's teaching on the issues of contraception, infertility treatments, sterilization and abortion under the guise of being helpful. Instead they are refusing the challenge of parenting their suffering children. They apply a quick-fix solution that contravenes the will of God and harms the souls of all involved.

If you are guilty of this, it is not too late to repent to the Lord and that child for misleading him or her. God's grace knows no bounds: He can bring good out of evil and redeem any situation. Trust in him to restore you, your children and your family.

In Sickness

I need a servant's heart toward sick people. When someone is sick in my home, I struggle to communicate compassion. I tend to fulfill duties: Get the person to the doctor, get the right medication and send him or her to bed so I can get on with my day. Instead I should see this as an opportunity to serve a particular family member. I should be grateful that I can love that person in a special way that day.

In the marriage vow we commit ourselves to genuinely caring for one another when we are ill. Part of growing in holiness now is to prepare us for suffering later. We have no idea what temporary disabilities or chronic illnesses will do to our spouse and to us as caregivers. There are many temptations in the midst of suffering: to indulge in self-pity, to be overly sensitive to criticism, to blame God, to doubt God's care for us or for our loved ones, to despair. It is critical for us to meet the challenges of suffering that arise early in marriage so that we are prepared for more difficult challenges down the road. This way we build spiritual stamina for the future and guard our hearts against the temptations of euthanasia and suicide.

Consider Job's wife. She lost everything that Job lost: seven sons and three daughters, all of their flocks, all of their crops and all of their servants. Her grief had to be extremely intense—a separate but real grief. We do not know the extent of her faith, but we do know of Job's, for Satan referred to his righteousness in his request to test him.

Job's response to his trials was to worship the Lord, even in the midst of his grief: "Then Job arose, and tore his robe, and shaved his head, and fell upon the ground, and worshiped. And he said, 'Naked I came from my mother's womb, and naked shall I return; the LORD gave, and the LORD has taken away; blessed be the name of the LORD'" (Job 1:20–21).

Then God allowed Satan to attack Job's physical health. "So Satan went forth from the presence of the LORD, and afflicted Job with loathsome sores from the sole of his foot to the crown of his head" (Job 2:7). Once Job was struck with boils, his suffering intensified.

At this point Job's wife succumbed to despair. She accused her beloved of worthless faith: "Do you still hold fast your integrity? Curse God, and die" (Job 2:9). Instead of drawing close to Job, helping him with his suffering and alleviating at least the emotional component, she increased his suffering. The only one Job had left in the world turned against him and tried to turn his heart against the Lord.

Who can comprehend the magnitude of loss each of these people faced? Though we understand how someone could despair, we know Job's wife's response shows a failure to have faith in God and to be faithful to her spouse. She should have helped Job bear the burden; she should have been the channel of grace that he so desperately needed. She should have cried out to the Lord for assistance instead of refusing to assist her beloved in his anguish.

Despair is a mortal sin; we must not succumb to this temptation, for the sake of our souls and the souls around us. A false compassion would end someone's suffering under the guise of mercy killing, for example, rather than bear the burden of suffering with him or her. God's grace will work through us in the midst of our suffering and the suffering of our loved ones, if we are open to it.

Job's response is the rebuke of a godly husband who speaks God's word to his wife, hopefully drawing her heart back to the Lord in truth and away from despair: "'You speak as one of the foolish women would speak. Shall we receive good at the hand of God, and shall we not receive evil?' In all this Job did not sin with his lips" (Job 2:10). He assured his wife that God was still in control and could be trusted in the midst of horrible affliction.

By the end of the book of Job, the Lord has restored every blessing Job enjoyed before the affliction, including seven more sons and three more daughters. Since there is no mention of the death of Job's wife or of any additional wives, I believe that Job's rebuke of his wife accomplished what Job intended: She repented of her sin of despair and was restored, to continue as his helpmate to reestablish their family.

We need to guard our hearts against the temptations of suffering, especially at the end of life. That is why, in the rosary, we pray for Mary's help "now and at the hour of our death." We know we need grace now, and we know we will need grace for a holy death, whenever that will be.

We have seen and heard about very holy people who have endured intense suffering to the end. Think of the example of Pope John Paul the Great, who endured the humiliation of suffering in public. He taught us not only how to live but also how to die. He showed us through suffering how to draw close to Christ and his agony on the cross. He exemplified a holy person who suffers well and offers strength and grace to others.

The saints echo Saint Paul's words to the believers in Colossae, "Now I rejoice in my sufferings for your sake, and in my flesh I complete what is lacking in

Christ's afflictions for the sake of his body, that is, the Church" (Colossians 1:24). This is part of the mystery of suffering: There is nothing inadequate about Christ's afflictions on our behalf; however, he has truly made us his body, his bride, so our afflictions united to the cross have salvific power.

This is the logic behind the phrase "Offer it up" when it comes to suffering. We have to be careful not to use these words to silence our children's complaints. If they understand what they are being asked to do, they can turn their suffering into powerful intercessory prayer.

And in Health

Practically we provide nutritional food to sustain the body and give strength. This involves meal planning, shopping, preparing and cooking with a thoughtful sense of balance. Physically our goal is not to look like teenagers—it is OK to look as if you had a baby if you did—but to be healthy. We want to take care of our bodies so that we can serve our families ably and live to know our grandchildren and great-grandchildren.

This vow also involves serving meals with genuine love. "Better is a dinner of herbs where love is / than a fatted ox and hatred with it" (Proverbs 15:17). When there is tension at the table, people do not feel hungry; but when the house is full of love, even a simple meal becomes a feast. Our words contribute to health.

"Pleasant words are like a honeycomb, / sweetness to the soul and health to the body" (Proverbs 16:24).

Around my family's dinner table we share "good things." This means everyone tells of something good that has happened since supper the night before. Sharing good news refreshes us physically and aids digestion. This is helpful in a large family, where multiple conversations can dominate a meal. It keeps conversation positive, gives everyone (no matter how small) a chance to share and lets all know we take them seriously. On Sundays we record each person's "good thing of the week." This has become a prized record of the events of the year.

For Richer, for Poorer

When it comes to finances, a young couple preparing for marriage may feel as if "love is all we need." The confrontation of such naïveté with reality can be harsh.

Saint Paul presents contentment as the goal: "There is great gain in godliness with contentment; for we brought nothing into the world, and we cannot take anything out of the world; but if we have food and clothing, with these we shall be content" (1 Timothy 6:6–8). He goes on to warn us of the temptations money offers:

> Those who desire to be rich fall into temptation, into a snare, into many senseless and hurtful desires that plunge men into ruin and destruction. For the love

147

of money is the root of all evils; it is through
this craving that some have wandered away from
the faith and pierced their hearts with many pangs.
(1 Timothy 6:9–10)

I spoke previously about the importance of a budget
for a family. Budgets help people sacrifice immediate
wants for long-term goals. They provide a framework
for saving for graduate school, a home, a new business
and children's college expenses. Planning and saving
go hand in hand with trusting in the Lord.

The husband's and wife's backgrounds may yield
varying estimations of what constitutes abundance
and what is enough for financial security. As a couple
discusses financial concerns, they build trust. Older
people may have to reassess their finances once they
have to rely on pensions. And those with married
children need to consider how they can bless their children without interfering with their children's financial
independence.

Scott and I encourage married couples to think,
pray and communicate about their financial goals.
How can they live within their means rather than
acquire debt? If they are blessed financially, what do
they hope to accomplish for the Lord? The goal is not
acquiring wealth for its own sake but being a good
steward of the resources he makes available to us.
Jesus reminds us in the parable of the talents that the

faithful steward is given greater resources to oversee (see Matthew 25:14–30).

Saint Paul refers elsewhere to the principle of contentment: "Not that I complain of want; for I have learned, in whatever state I am, to be content. I know how to be abased, and I know how to abound; in any and all circumstances I have learned the secret of facing plenty and hunger, abundance and want" (Philippians 4:11–12).

It sounds strange to speak of being content with a lot as well as a little, but the point is that we should trust God to give us what we need. It is Christ, not the resources, who strengthens us. We pursue godliness rather than financial gain so that we love God and use money, rather than the other way around.

For Better or for Worse

Each spouse bears with the failings and weaknesses of the other. "We who are strong ought to bear with the failings of the weak, and not to please ourselves" (Romans 15:1). We differentiate here between sins, which need to change, and weaknesses—poor habits, idiosyncrasies, poor manners—that may not necessarily change to accommodate us (however nice that would be).

Weaknesses include the hormonal challenges that women have related to fertility. Pregnancy, delivery, infertility, miscarriage or stillbirth and PMS can all affect a woman emotionally. A word to the wisehusband: Factor in the difficulty without reminding your wife that you are doing so.

We women cannot excuse bad behavior on the basis of hormonal difficulties. We must take responsibility for our thoughts, emotional equilibrium, words and actions. At the same time, if we feel overwhelmed by certain emotions, we may need to take care of ourselves—perhaps by drinking more fluids, eating better, getting more rest or hiring a sitter so we can "take a day off." These measures can limit our temptations and others' difficulties with us. Even in times of stress and weakness, we can still be channels of grace.

We all cause small irritations as we share life: socks strewn on the floor, hair left in the bathroom sink, small bits of trash on the floor near the trash receptacle (which temporarily functioned as a basketball hoop), the cap left off the toothpaste tube or the toilet seat left up. For the sake of a loving home, we need to say what irritates us, learn what we do that bothers the other and determine how to live with the things that will not change.

First Corinthians 13:5 reminds us, "Love does not insist on its own way; it is not irritable or resentful." As a friend who was recently widowed said, "The absence of those little irritations is one of my reminders that he is gone."

The Church has chosen Colossians 3:12–21 to be read in Year A on the Feast of the Holy Family, and she also recommends it as a New Testament reading at weddings. This passage has special significance for Scott and me, because my father chose to preach on it at our wedding and the weddings of my siblings. The passage reminds us of the virtues and actions that will help our family imitate the Holy Family:

> Put on then, as God's chosen ones, holy and beloved, compassion, kindness, lowliness, meekness, and patience, forbearing one anothe...forgiving each other; as the Lord has forgiven you, so you also must forgive. And over all these put on love, which binds everything together in perfect harmony. And let the peace of Christ rule in your hearts, to which indeed you were called in the one body. And be thankful. Let the word of Christ dwell in you richly, as you teach and admonish one another in all wisdom, and as you sing psalms and hymns and spiritual songs with thankfulness in your hearts to God. And whatever you do, in word or deed, do everything in the name of the Lord Jesus, giving thanks to God the Father through him. (Colossians 3:12–17)

We have access to the Prince of Peace. If we let him rule in our hearts, his peace will reign in our homes. Then we will do good and not harm to those who dwell with us.

CHAPTER TEN

Conflict Resolution

An elderly priest visited a second-grade religion class and asked, "What did Jesus teach about marriage?"

At first the little ones gave him blank looks. Then a boy in the front row shot up his hand. "Jesus said, 'Father, forgive them—they know not what they do!'"

Married life is a journey for bride and groom into uncharted lands, with many highs and lows. They discover strengths they did not know they had, they uncover weaknesses they feared they had, and they find that God's grace is sufficient for the journey. For each this path includes a cross, a daily dying to self for the love of God and spouse in imitation of Jesus' sacrificial life (see Mark 8:34). Each has interior struggles with sin, and there are conflicts between them. Yet the Lord guides them so that good and not harm result. Even falls can become upward falls with grace.

The Power of Anger

Anger and love are passions that express "I care." But passions are like fire. We talk of "burning love" and "in the heat of anger." We need self-control with passionate love, but do we realize how much we also need self-control with anger?

Anger can motivate toward good. It can strengthen our courage to defend a family member and motivate us to fight injustice, as does MADD (Mothers Against Drunk Drivers). Yet anger can cause danger and destruction. Saint Paul cautions, "Be angry but do not sin" (Ephesians 4:26a; Psalm 4:4). This is a difficult call.

Anger is the most troublesome emotion in family life. It can make a home a place of tension, conflict, defensiveness, hurt and even abuse. "A hot-tempered man stirs up strife, / but he who is slow to anger quiets contention" (Proverbs 15:18). Saint Paul specifically warns husbands in this regard, "Love your wives, and do not be harsh with them" (Colossians 3:19).

It is important to consider how we express anger. Do we communicate effectively about the conflict we feel? Do we resolve conflict, or do we just stay quiet and seethe, dreading confrontation? Do we vacillate between being people-pleasers and being persons of conviction?

We approach marriage from a particular family system complete with rules about conflict resolution. No family is perfect: We are all fruit of Adam's dysfunctional family tree. Some learned behaviors need to change. By God's grace we can incorporate the strengths from our families and then improve on them. Our goal is to communicate respect in the midst of conflict.

When Words Are Many

We choose to get angry, though rarely without provocation. We hear criticism and react. We begin an argument late at night and are too tired to think before we speak. We complain to someone who is not feeling well and are drawn into a quarrel, when all we wanted was some sympathy. When either of us is weak physically, we may not have a lot of grace between us to handle friction, and then there are sparks.

"When words are many, transgression is not lacking, / but he who restrains his lips is prudent" (Proverbs 10:19). It would help if we had a neon sign that regularly flashed, "All thoughts are not worth saying!"

When it comes to words, we need self-control, a fruit of the Spirit. "There is one whose rash words are like sword thrusts, / but the tongue of the wise brings healing" (Proverbs 12:18). We may feel the pain of rash words, but we always have a choice as to whether or not we respond in kind. Wise words bring healing if we stop in the midst of conflict and choose to speak them. "A soft answer turns away wrath, / but a harsh word stirs up anger" (Proverbs 15:1).

Look at the contrast between a man without self-control and one who has cultivated it: "A man without self-control / is like a city broken into and left without walls" (Proverbs 25:28). "He who is slow to anger is better than the mighty, / and he who rules his spirit than he who takes a city" (Proverbs 16:32). From these verses we see the power of a man's self-control to impart security to those near him.

Women, avoid a man given to anger, or you may find yourself imitating him. Worse yet, you may find his anger directed against you and your children (see Proverbs 22:24–25). Anger is not manly; self-control is.

In the midst of conflict we should remember that "the wise of heart is called a man of discernment, / and pleasant speech increases persuasiveness" (Proverbs 16:21). This is not a competition with a winner and a loser but a team pulling together. When we find ourselves pushing against one another, we may need a brief time apart to cool down and to pray for discernment. This is *not* the silent treatment; it is silent space in which grace can operate more freely. "He who restrains his words has knowledge, / and he who has a cool spirit is a man of understanding" (Proverbs 17:27).

On the one hand, we do not have to correct everything. "Good sense makes a man slow to anger, / and it is his glory to overlook an offense" (Proverbs 19:11). On the other hand, unresolved conflicts can simmer below the surface and then emerge in an unpredictable way, like a beach ball held under water that pops out in a random direction. Through prayer and reflection we discern what resolution is needed.

Often a wife has a greater sense than her husband that reconciliation is needed, either between them or between Dad and one of the children. We need right relationships on the human level to be able to worship the Lord. If we have something against someone or someone has something against us, we are to leave our gift at the altar and initiate reconciliation (see Matthew 5:23–24; 18:15–17). Through Christ God has given us "the ministry of reconciliation" (2 Corinthians 5:18). We can build right relationships in our families.

Peace Initiative: The Strategy

Conflicts occur in marriage, no matter how spiritual we are. The goal is life in the peaceful zone with occasional conflicts, rather than life in the war zone with occasional détente.

It takes work to figure out fair rules of engagement, but it is necessary. If when all is calm we agree to certain rules for a fair fight, we are more likely to use them in the heat of battle. This is some of the most important work we do in the first year of marriage, but it is also a lifelong challenge, because we will be growing in grace till the end. Here are some steps toward peaceful resolutions:

Prayer. We need insight and wisdom to know what difficulties need to be discussed and when. We need supernatural protection, so that we will not say or do hurtful things to one another. We ask our guardian angels to work so that good and not harm will result from our disagreements. Even in the midst of conflict, we should pray the Saint Michael prayer and request protection from heaven against the forces of evil that want to tear apart a godly marriage and family. We also need to pray that God will unite our hearts, minds and wills.

Trust. We begin with the premise that we are *for* each other: We are on the same team. We attack the problem together rather than attack each other. We look for insights we each have, and we ask ourselves how we are contributing to the conflict. Our goal should not be to set the other person straight but to share our hearts so that together we can solve a problem.

Speak the truth in love to impart grace. We must communicate with respect: it is not only *what* we share but also *how* we share it that demonstrates real love. We should avoid labeling, belittling, sarcasm, insults, words of condemnation, name-calling and swearing. "Let no evil talk come out of your mouths, but only such as is good for edifying, as fits the occasion, that it may impart grace to those who hear" (Ephesians 4:29).

Drop always *and* never *from conflict vocabulary.* We always get in trouble with accusations that are never true. Sometimes we overstate something and then react emotionally, as if it were true. This can escalate an argument.

We need humility. We only see part of any situation. Our insight can be useful, but we also need our spouse's insight. We want God's best for our marriage, and that means examining our own feelings, flaws, fears and failures. We need to be ready to accuse ourselves and to excuse our spouse. We also want to avoid comparisons with parents, siblings and others.

Timing is important. Ephesians 4:26 states, "Do not let the sun go down on your anger." In other words, try to resolve conflicts that day, keeping short accounts with your loved one. (Having conflicts resolved certainly helps you sleep better.) This command, however, has to be balanced with common sense. Late at night probably is not a suitable time to begin a discussion. The more tired we are, the more we struggle with self-control over thoughts, feelings and words. Hunger and hormones also can increase the stress level. Be prudent in deciding when to resolve conflict.

Pick your battles carefully. Avoid the attitude of "peace at any price"; it's too expensive. Real peace is not appeasement but the result of clear communication. It takes work. At the same time, resist an argumentative spirit; do not become quarrelsome or contentious. It can degenerate into conflict for conflict's sake and accomplish little else than heartache.

Be thankful, even in the midst of conflict, for God is at work. "Count it all joy, my brethren, when you meet various trials, for you know that the testing of your faith produces steadfastness. And let steadfastness have its full effect, that you may be perfect and complete, lacking in nothing" (James 1:2–3). Conflict and resolution play a role in perfecting each of us.

If you reach an impasse, try not to react negatively. Do not indulge door slamming, the silent treatment or withdrawal from intimacy. Excluding the other person does not resolve anything. A brief time apart (minutes, not hours), requested as gently and respectfully as possible, lessens the probability of saying something you will regret later. It gives you a moment to pray for more light, to ask God's help for clarity, to pray for the other person (with thanksgiving!) and to try to see the other person's perspective. Then get back together as soon as possible to resolve the conflict.

Argue in private. There is no good reason to expose your children to the pain of confrontation. They can and should be taught about conflict resolution but in a different context. If it cannot be helped—you are all in the car or a hotel room together—find a way to curtail the discussion and allow uncomfortable silence until a more opportune time arises to complete the discussion. It will not be pleasant, but it will not be as unpleasant as making your children absorb angry words between you.

Allow the past to be past. Forget what you have forgiven. Allow your spouse the fresh start you want him to give you. You will continue to grow in grace as new creations in Christ. The best is yet to come!

Where Are You on the Anger Ladder?

All of us, including Jesus, experience anger. We do not stop feeling anger just because we are Christians. The question is, "How can we express anger in the most constructive way?"

Gary Chapman and Dr. Ross Campbell's "Anger Ladder" is a helpful tool for identifying incremental steps from destructive to constructive expressions of anger.[1] Note that the phrases in capital letters indicate positive ways to express anger.

To use the ladder, identify the rung you are on now, and look at the step above it to see how to improve your conflict resolution pattern. Also identify patterns of conflict from your family system, and realize changes you need to make to strengthen relationships.

We determine our approach: "This is the way I am," *or* "I can mature in my responses." If we want our home characterized by peace rather than conflict, we can take steps in anger management and conflict resolution for the well-being of our family. We *can* mature.

THE ANGER LADDER

POSITIVE

1. PLEASANT • SEEKING RESOLUTION • FOCUSING ANGER ON SOURCE • HOLDING TO PRIMARY COMPLAINT • THINKING LOGICALLY

2. PLEASANT • FOCUSING ANGER ON SOURCE • HOLDING TO PRIMARY COMPLAINT • THINKING LOGICALLY

POSITIVE AND NEGATIVE

3. FOCUSING ANGER ON SOURCE • HOLDING TO PRIMARY COMPLAINT • THINKING LOGICALLY • unpleasant, loud

4. HOLDING TO PRIMARY COMPLAINT • THINKING LOGICALLY • unpleasant, loud • displacing anger to other sources

5. FOCUSING ANGER ON SOURCE • HOLDING TO PRIMARY COMPLAINT • THINKING LOGICALLY • unpleasant, loud • verbal abuse

6. THINKING LOGICALLY • unpleasant, loud • displacing anger to other sources • expressing unrelated complaints

PRIMARILY NEGATIVE

7. unpleasant, loud • displacing anger to other sources • expressing unrelated complaints • emotionally destructive behavior

8. unpleasant, loud • displacing anger to other sources • expressing unrelated complaints • verbal abuse • emotionally destructive behavior

9. unpleasant, loud • cursing • displacing anger to other sources • expressing unrelated complaints • verbal abuse • emotionally destructive behavior

10. FOCUSING ANGER ON SOURCE • unpleasant, loud • cursing • displacing anger to other sources • throwing objects • emotionally destructive behavior

11. unpleasant, loud • cursing • displacing anger to other sources • throwing objects • emotionally destructive behavior

NEGATIVE

12. FOCUSING ANGER ON SOURCE • unpleasant, loud • cursing • destroying property • verbal abuse • emotionally destructive behavior

13. unpleasant, loud • cursing • displacing anger to other sources • destroying property • verbal abuse • emotionally destructive behavior

14. unpleasant, loud • cursing • displacing anger to other sources • destroying property • verbal abuse • physical abuse • emotionally destructive behavior

15. passive-aggressive behavior

Notice that the most dangerous stage, according to Dr. Campbell, is passive-aggressive behavior. Here someone does not deal with conflict or even acknowledge that there is conflict. The person appears to be peaceful but is actually seething inside. Then, all of a sudden, the anger comes out sideways. The response can be volcanic, and it usually leaves others to deal with the fallout. No resolution is possible if the passive-aggressive person continues in that mode. He or she doesn't have a problem; you do! He or she doesn't need counseling; you do!

Look to Jesus

Forgiveness is critical to conflict resolution in marriage. Forgiveness does not depend on feeling forgiving; rather it is a matter of the will, determining to extend forgiveness and asking the Lord to help our emotions line up with our actions.

We see a powerful example of this in the life of Corrie ten Boom, a Christian whose family harbored Jews from the Nazis in Holland until someone betrayed them. Corrie, her sister and her father were arrested and sent to a concentration camp, where her sister and father died. Many years later Corrie spoke to an audience in Germany, and the very guard who had been involved in her sister's death approached her, thanking her for her talk and asking her for forgiveness for what he had done.

When the guard extended his hand, everything in Corrie's being recoiled. Then she prayed that Christ would forgive him through her, and she extended her hand. In that act Christ flooded Corrie with forgiveness for this man who had been the instrument of such cruelty and suffering for her. Christ loved him through her and forgave him through her. Christ can and will do this for us, if we ask.

What can we do when we remember sins committed against us that we have forgiven? We can thank God that we have forgiven that person. This is humility: to choose to forget and, when we cannot forget, to choose to continue to forgive. After all, with every Our Father we directly tie our request for forgiveness to the forgiveness we extend to others: "And forgive us our trespasses, / As we forgive those who trespass against us." After teaching his disciples this prayer, Jesus added, "For if you forgive men their trespasses, your heavenly Father also will forgive you; but if you do not forgive men their trespasses, neither will your Father forgive your trespasses" (Matthew 6:12, 14–15).

In all this we can extend to our children a beautiful model of Christian living. We cannot expect them to control their anger and other emotions better than we do. We can share the Anger Ladder with older children, so they can improve their anger management and help the family express anger in a more constructive way. And when we blow it, we can give them the example of asking for forgiveness, resolving to do better and praying for change.

Even in the midst of conflict, God calls us to be thankful, for he "is at work in [us], both to will and to work for his good pleasure" (Philippians 2:13). He wants to heal us and to restore relationships. This is difficult for us to see when we focus on the difficulties before us, but it is possible if we keep our eyes fixed on Jesus.

Thankfulness does not depend on our temperament: Though some people may find it easier to be upbeat, everyone is commanded to acknowledge God's work in their lives with thanks. Neither does it depend on getting what we want: Sometimes our will coincides with God's—relish the coincidence—but when things do not go our way, God is *still* in control, and for that we give thanks.

No one can make us happy or make us sad: Those are our choices. And no one can rob us of joy, even in the midst of suffering. "Rejoice always, pray constantly, give thanks in all circumstances; for this is the will of God in Christ Jesus for you" (1 Thessalonians 5:16–18). No matter what is happening in our vocation, we give thanks to the Lord.

We Desire and Nurture Unity

When we desire to honor the Lord in embracing his design for marriage, we know there will be difficulties.

It is as if we have painted a bull's-eye on our back. There will be evil spiritual resistance against our plan for a godly marriage and family. So we need godly resistance to move our plan forward.

We resist the world's temptation to compare ourselves to others or our marriage to theirs. We resist the flesh—our desires, strength, rights, will—acknowledging that we still struggle with concupiscence. And we resist the devil, who uses our faults, weaknesses and sins against us, striving to pit us against our loved ones.

Kindness from the Lord nurtures repentance and change in us. "Do you not know that God's kindness is meant to lead you to repentance?" (Romans 2:4). This is a good strategy for us to have with our loved ones. We bear with each other's faults, failings and weaknesses, always remembering that success in family life is faithfulness, not perfection.

Some people experience a kind of "dark night of the soul" in marriage, offering selfless love without the consolation of feelings of love toward or from a spouse. Pray for perseverance! "We rejoice in our sufferings, knowing that suffering produces endurance, and endurance produces character, and character produces hope, and hope does not disappoint us, because God's love has been poured into our hearts through the Holy Spirit who has been given to us" (Romans 5:3–5).

Draw on the power of the Holy Spirit to do through you what you cannot do on your own, to be hope-filled even in the midst of suffering. The *Catechism* points out that we can count on this help: "The Holy Spirit is the seal of their covenant, the ever-available source of their love and the strength to renew their fidelity" (*CCC*, 1624).

Does building a godly marriage and family seem overwhelming—beyond your capacity? It is! But the good news is that God gives us the grace we need to be faithful to our vocation. And he will do this work because he wants us to have godly marriages and godly children.

God *is* able to work in and through us, so that even in conflicts we can do good and not harm to each other. "Now to him who by the power at work within us is able to do far more abundantly than all that we ask or think, to him be glory in the Church and in Christ Jesus to all generations, for ever and ever. Amen" (Ephesians 3:20–21).

PART SIX

All the Days of Her Life
Proverbs 31:12b

CHAPTER ELEVEN

Faithful Now and Always

She does him good, and not harm, / all the days of her life" (Proverbs 31:12). The commitment to faithfulness encompasses a woman's whole life: before marriage, during marriage and in widowhood.

All the Days...Before Marriage

Even before a woman knows whom she will marry, she can honor him by her thoughts, words and actions. Saint Francis de Sales cautions, "If you look to married life in this life, guard your first love jealously for your husband. It seems to me a miserable fraud to give a husband a worn-out heart, whose love has been frittered away and despoiled of its first bloom instead of a true, wholehearted love."[1]

If you have not yet found your future spouse, use this time to prepare yourself to be a wonderful gift for the one God intends for you. Remember too that a person with whom you are romantically involved now may be someone else's future spouse, so respect that potential commitment appropriately.

These days also include the pursuit of purity in the midst of an honorable courtship with your chosen one.

Be ready to embrace the commitment of marriage if this is God's call for your life.

All the Days...During Marriage

I grew up in a family where marriage vows were taken very seriously and faithfulness was assumed. As I prepared to go to church on my wedding day, Mom stopped me for a moment and said, "I want to tell you something. You can still change your mind. But once you are married, your home is with him. If you are at odds with each other, you cannot come here. In that sense, this is no longer your home."

Wow! That was clear. Mom was not questioning my choice in marrying Scott. She simply wanted me to understand what a permanent decision this was. (What a contrast to parents who assure their children that their home will always be a place of refuge if things become difficult!) I am so grateful for this clear boundary. When Scott became Catholic and I had no intention of doing so, I struggled with staying in our marriage. But I knew that even if my parents might side with me theologically, they would never let me just walk back in the door. They knew it was essential for us to work through our dilemma, and they counseled us and assisted us toward that end.

Faithfulness in marriage is a conscious choice, an active effort to guard marital chastity and embrace fidelity. We choose purity in our thoughts, words and deeds. We reject all thought of adultery. We embrace our husbands in generous fruitfulness (see CCC, 8), contrary to our culture's rejection of children through contraception, sterilization and abortion.

All the Days...After Marriage

Many of us will face the death of our spouse. The Lord is the "protector of widows" (Psalm 68:5), for "he upholds the widow and the fatherless" (Psalm 146:9). The Lord takes care of women who have been left through death or abandonment.

How does a wife continue to honor a spouse who has died? She speaks well of him at all times, honoring the legacy he has left. She has Masses said on his behalf and prays for the repose of his soul. If there is money to do so, she may give a donation in his name or establish a scholarship or award as an ongoing tribute to him.

The Christian widow continues to draw her children close to their father through remembrances and thanksgiving. She encourages her children to share memories and photos so that they will be able to help their children appreciate their grandfather.

This strengthens the family and helps the younger generations trust the Lord whenever they encounter grief.

Paul offers this advice to the widow considering remarriage: "A wife is bound to her husband as long as he lives. If the husband dies, she is free to be married to whom she wishes, only in the Lord" (1 Corinthians 7:39). Thus the goals of a new marriage will be committed love and the common pursuit of God's will.

Divorce Unveiled

The priests of the old covenant lament that God is not answering their prayers or accepting their sacrifices. The prophet Malachi explains the situation: God will not answer their prayers because of their marital infidelity.

> You ask, "Why does he not?" Because the LORD was witness to the covenant between you and the wife of your youth, to whom you have been faithless, though she is your companion and your wife by covenant. Has not the one God made and sustained for us the spirit of life? And what does he desire? Godly offspring. So take heed to yourselves, and let none be faithless to the wife of his youth. "For I hate divorce, says the LORD the God of Israel, and covering one's garment with violence, says the LORD of hosts. So take heed to yourselves and do not be faithless." (Malachi 2:14–16)

Why does the Lord link his hatred for divorce and his hatred for violence? Divorce is violence against the marriage and against each spouse. It tries to tear apart what God has joined. Faithlessness to your spouse ruins your marriage and your relationship with God. Reconciliation and repentance is needed.

Wedding vows typically include "till *death* do us

part" and "as long as we both shall *live.*" These phrases highlight the fact that a couple is making a commitment for life. They understand that the marriage bond is indissoluble. However, two couples who wed in a Protestant church altered their vow to accommodate a different view. One couple promised, "Till *divorce* do us part." The other couple vowed, "As long as we both shall *love.*" How long might that be?

My parents had their first marital tiff as they stepped onto the aisle to exit the church after their wedding. Dad reached for Mom's hand to escort her, but she dropped his hand to pick up her skirt. A little miffed, he reached more decisively for her hand, and she pulled her hand away again to grasp her hoop skirt. By the time they exited the church, he was angry.

"Why did you humiliate me in front of all those people?"

Mom had her reason. "I'm not used to a hoop skirt. I had to hold it up with both hands, or I would have fallen flat on my face, which would have embarrassed both of us a whole lot more!"

With that explanation the spat was over. Both understood the other person's actions. The moment of anger passed, and the feeling of love returned. But a vow based on "feeling love" for each other, rather than a commitment to each other, would be very sandy ground on which to build a home.

The Pharisees' Trap

> Now when Jesus had finished these sayings, he went
> away from Galilee and entered the region of Judea
> beyond the Jordan; and large crowds followed him,
> and he healed them there. And Pharisees came up to
> him and tested him by asking, "Is it lawful to divorce
> one's wife for any cause?" (Matthew 19:1–3)

Why does Saint Matthew mention the region of Judea
beyond the Jordan? This is where King Herod lived,
where John the Baptist preached against adultery
before his arrest. King Herod had him arrested because
John declared that anyone who married his brother's
wife, which is exactly what King Herod had done, was
an adulterer. The issues of marriage, remarriage, adultery and civil divorce were the cause of John the
Baptist's imprisonment and death.

This also happens to be the location where Moses
gave the Deuteronomic law to the Israelites, including
the laws dealing with remarriage and adultery (see
Deuteronomy 5:18; 22:22; 24:1–4). Jesus, the new
Moses, is about to repeal that law and reveal God's
original design.

The Jewish leaders do not ask Jesus about divorce
and remarriage because they respect his wisdom. Nor
are they asking him to settle a dispute between two
current rabbinic schools of thought on this matter.
They are trying to test him on a matter that, should

he answer the wrong way, could get him into very significant trouble.

There were two major schools of thought among rabbis relative to divorce. Rabbi Shammai held the strict legal view that adultery presented the only possible case for legitimate divorce and remarriage. Rabbi Hillel taught the unpopular liberal view of no-fault divorce: In essence, if a wife burned breakfast, the man could have a new wife by lunch.

Why are the Pharisees trying to test Jesus? They want to trap him so they can destroy him. If Jesus takes the strict legal view, the Pharisees might alert King Herod's guards. Agreeing with the liberal view, on the other hand, will discredit him in the eyes of the common people.

Jesus gives an unexpected response: *no* divorce *and* remarriage. He takes a position *no one* promotes, including Moses! Even John the Baptist, in denouncing Herod's adultery, did not question Moses' teaching on divorce and remarriage. The Pharisees are incredulous.

The Reeducation of the Teachers of the Law

Jesus responds to their incredulity:

> Have you not read that he who made them from the beginning made them male and female, and said, "For this reason a man shall leave his father and mother and be joined to his wife, and the two shall become

one"? So they are no longer two but one. What therefore God has joined together, let no man put asunder. (Matthew 19:4–6)

Jesus answers this elite group of scholars, who have invested their lives in understanding and teaching the Law, by referring to Genesis with "Have you not read...?" This is like a lawyer approaching the Supreme Court and saying, "Remember the Constitution? It's really interesting; it starts with 'We the people...'."

Jesus is saying, in essence, let's review the ABCs: Let's look at Genesis. This rebuke would have cut to the core of the Pharisees' pride.

First, Jesus highlights, from Genesis 1, that man was created male and female in God's image; second, from Genesis 2, that the two become one flesh in their marriage. Jesus challenges the Pharisees: If God has joined two people, can *you* separate them? Divorce is not a part of the plan from the beginning. Jesus restores the dignity of man and woman in marriage as God instituted it in creation.

Throughout the Old Testament God proclaims his unconditional love and faithfulness for his people in marital terms. Though their idolatry is described as adulterous against him, he is faithful. Jesus has come to fulfill God's pledge as the Bridegroom laying down his life for his bride, the Church. Further, Jesus elevates marriage to a new level, that of a sacrament, making it a living witness of the relationship between Christ and the Church. Jesus calls Christian couples to participate in the same indissolubility that binds Christ to his bride.

What God Has Joined

Marriage is not a man-made institution: The state is not uniting two people; God is. Unity is not simply the goal but the reality of marriage, and that unity is divinely instituted. Neither a legal decree nor a consensus of society can nullify it. The state can declare a civil divorce as a formal separation, but it cannot alter the reality of the couple's marriage. A state that assumes the power to nullify a marriage oversteps its bounds and damages the foundation of society.

Children exemplify the unity between a man and woman in marriage. How can that which has become one ever become two again? What part of the child is the mother's? What part is the father's? Who can separate what God has joined?

Pope John Paul the Great wrote:

Being rooted in the personal and total self-giving of the couple, and being required by the good of the children, the indissolubility of marriage finds its ultimate truth in the plan that God has manifested in His revelation. He wills and He communicates the indissolubility of marriage as a fruit, a sign, and a requirement of the absolutely faithful love that God has for man and that the Lord Jesus has for the Church.[2]

Jesus wants to draw people's hearts back to God's original design.

What Did Moses Teach?

The Pharisees object to Jesus' interpretation: "Why then did Moses command one to give a certificate of divorce, and to put her away?" (Matthew 19:7). They are referring to Deuteronomy 24:1–4:

> When a man takes a wife and marries her, if then she finds no favor in his eyes because he has found some indecency in her, and he writes her a bill of divorce and puts it in her hand and sends her out of his house, and she departs out of his house, and if she goes and becomes another man's wife, and the latter husband dislikes her and writes her a bill of divorce and puts it in her hand and sends her out of his house, or if the latter husband dies, who took her to be his wife, then her former husband, who sent her away, may not take her again to be his wife, after she has been defiled; for that is an abomination before the LORD, and you shall not bring guilt upon the land which the LORD your God gives you for an inheritance.

What is Moses teaching? A husband could repudiate his wife but not vice versa. He could write a bill of divorce so that the repudiated wife could remarry, though she could never remarry her first husband after a death or divorce of the second. This was to protect a woman's dignity against being treated as property. If she was to be abandoned, the husband had to free her to remarry.

Moses is neither commanding divorce nor condoning it. He is presenting complex case law dealing with indecency found in a wife, allowing for divorce and remarriage but not requiring it. Jesus emphasizes this: "For your hardness of heart Moses allowed you to divorce your wives, but from the beginning it was not so" (Matthew 19:8). Moses' case law does not abrogate God's original intent for marriage.

Catch the irony? Who had a hard heart? Obviously, Pharaoh did (see Exodus 4; 14) but Jesus is saying that the people of Israel *also* struggled with hardness of heart. (Moses had an easier time getting the Israelites out of Egypt than getting Egypt out of the people of Israel.) Jesus' phrase "*your* hardness of heart" includes the Pharisees of the present with the Israelites of the past. They also have closed their hearts to God's truth about marriage.

What Does Jesus Teach?

Saint Luke records Jesus' words: "Every one who divorces his wife and marries another commits adultery, and he who marries a woman divorced from her husband commits adultery" (Luke 16:18). There is no exception here, nor in the Gospel of Mark, where Jesus says, "Whoever divorces his wife and marries another, commits adultery against her; and if she divorces her husband and marries another, she commits adultery" (Mark 10:11–12).

In the Gospel of Matthew, Jesus addresses the Pharisees with the weight of his authority. "And I say to you: whoever divorces his wife, except for unchastity, and marries another, commits adultery; and he who marries a divorced woman, commits adultery" (Matthew 19:9). This exception clause has been the source of some confusion since the time of the Protestant Reformation. The phrase cannot be a direct contradiction of Jesus' teaching in both Luke and Mark, binding early believers' consciences to contrary teachings. Jesus cannot contradict himself, nor does Scripture contradict itself.

With that in mind, what does the phrase "except for unchastity" mean? *Unchastity* in Greek is the word *pornea*, which refers to sexual immorality: adultery, homosexuality and other forms of sexually aberrant behavior prohibited by the Church.

Two prominent views harmonize Jesus' teaching in Mark and Luke with the exception clause in Matthew. The *Patristic view* applies the exception clause to divorce but not to remarriage. In other words, sexual immorality could be legitimate grounds for divorce as a permanent separation, but remarriage would still result in adultery. Sexual immorality does not necessitate a divorce, for by the grace of God it is possible to forgive a spouse; under no circumstances does the Church require divorce. "Above all hold unfailing your love for one another, since love covers a multitude of sins" (1 Peter 4:8). Love can cover a multitude of sins, even though this would be extremely difficult.

In the *Levitical view*, the exception clause is referring to sexual sins that render a marriage invalid. In other words, marriage is possible following a civil divorce of an invalid marriage. This would be the biblical grounds for annulment. In that case, the marriage following a divorce would not be remarriage but a valid marriage. For example, in 1 Corinthians 5:1–2, the Greek word *pornea* is used to describe the unlawful union between a man and his father's wife.[4]

What Does Saint Paul Teach?

Saint Paul offers two options for a married couple who are separated: "To the married I give charge, not I but the Lord, that the wife should not separate from her husband (but if she does, let her remain single or else be reconciled to her husband)—and that the husband should not divorce his wife" (1 Corinthians 7:10–11). In other words, the couple can (1) remain separated and live as single people or (2) reconcile.

The Church acknowledges that there can be legitimate grounds for separation of "bed and board." In fact, a separation might be a necessity, such as in an abusive situation, where the safety of a spouse and children is at risk. Perhaps a civil divorce is necessary-for added protection and monetary aid. However, remarriage is not a possibility.

"A married woman is bound by law to her husband as long as he lives.... Accordingly, she will be called an adulteress if she lives with another man while her husband is alive" (Romans 7:2, 3). Saint Paul affirms that only death releases a husband and wife from their marriage vows.

Witness of the Disciples

"The disciples' incredulous response to Jesus confirms the Catholic Church's constant teaching on the indissolubility of sacramental marriage."[3] This response is, "If such is the case of a man with his wife, it is not expedient to marry" (Matthew 19:10).

Jesus does not weaken his teaching to make it more palatable. "Not all men can receive this precept, but only those to whom it is given" (Matthew 19:11). Then he teaches about consecrated life, by which God calls some to give themselves completely for the kingdom. Jesus' words apply to both marriage and consecrated celibacy: Faithfulness to the call can be difficult, yet it is possible by God's grace.

Divorce and Annulment

The Church applies Jesus' teaching to all marriages, not just Catholic marriages. Even a Protestant who has remarried after a divorce has to have that marriage validated before he or she receives the sacraments of initiation. It may seem offensive to delay receiving someone until the marriage issue is resolved, but the Church has to be faithful to our Lord.

If you are unmarried but the person in whom you are interested has been divorced without an annulment, you need to treat that individual as a married person. The presumption is that a person is validly married; the burden of proof is on the one seeking the annulment. Without an annulment a person should not date, let alone remarry, for "the remarried spouse is then in a situation of public and permanent adultery" (see CCC, 2384).

Trust the process to God, and let the Church confirm God's will for your relationship. Resist any temptation to downplay the role of the Church in this matter. Don't think, "In the 'eyes of the Church' he's married, but not in mine!" He is either married or not.

The Catholic Church cannot nullify a marriage bond; however, she has criteria to discern whether or not a valid marriage has occurred. A declaration of nullity can be pursued either for reason of a serious defect in the consent of one or both parties or a serious defect in what is called canonical form.[4] This is not Catholic-style divorce, though at times it appears like it, particularly in the United States, where the number of annulment applications exceeds those requested throughout the rest of the world each year.

A Church court receives a request for an annulment, assigns a defender of the bond (who assumes a valid marriage) and receives testimony. The ruling of the court is not infallible: The court is limited by the truthfulness of those giving testimony. However, a person may, with a clear conscience, act on the basis of the court's ruling. If the Church declares the marriage null, the persons involved are free to enter into valid marriages.

Often people express concern about the children from a union that has been declared null. Nullity has no bearing on children's status. They were conceived within a marriage presumed to be valid at the time. They are never treated as illegitimate.

Many people testify that the process of annulment is a healing process. Though it is difficult to examine painful parts of their lives, they experience the Church's care for them. This is another opportunity for the Church to demonstrate Jesus' teaching that the truth sets us free.

CHAPTER TWELVE

The Sanctity of Marriage

From its beginning Christianity, unlike other world religions, has required monogamy, yet many branches of Christianity accept divorce as a fact of life, allowing a kind of serial polygamy: more than one spouse but just one at a time. Various branches of the Orthodox Church allow reception of Communion after as many as three divorces and marriage to a fourth wife. Most of the twenty-six thousand Protestant denominations accept the state's authority to break a marriage, and most do not restrict communion. Though divorce is never encouraged, remarriage is allowed.

Christ's teaching on the indissolubility of marriage was not challenged until Erasmus presented a different view in the sixteenth century. In the years immediately following the Reformation, Protestant writers and theologians agreed that remarriage after divorce should be allowed, though they disagreed as to what constituted valid reasons. Luther, Melancthon and others even signed a letter to a German prince, Philip of Hesse, in 1539, encouraging him to consider polygamy with his mistress rather than continue in adultery.

Witness of the Church

The Catholic Church at the time of the Reformation and to the present maintains a unified teaching on marriage, divorce and remarriage. This teaching will remain the same: No amount of lobbying will change it, and no future pope will overturn it.

> This unequivocal insistence on the indissolubility of the marriage bond may have left some perplexed and could seem to be a demand impossible to realize.... By coming to restore the original order of creation disturbed by sin, [Jesus] himself gives the strength and grace to live marriage in the new dimension of the Reign of God. It is by following Christ, renouncing themselves, and taking up their crosses that spouses will be able to "receive" the original meaning of marriage and live it with the help of Christ. This grace of Christian marriage is a fruit of Christ's cross, the source of all Christian life. (*CCC*, 1615)

For centuries Christian people of all levels of intelligence, talent and wealth have lived this truth by the grace of God. Jesus gave his teaching on marriage in the midst of an "adulterous and sinful generation" (Mark 8:38; see Matthew 12:39), so the challenges that our day presents cannot be excuses to ignore the Church's teaching. Even nonreligious couples in many countries have remained faithful in marriage. How much more is faithfulness possible in a marriage empowered by sacramental grace?

Our loving heavenly Father gives us this teaching

on marriage to bless us rather than to make life difficult or even impossible. He establishes boundaries for marriage that enable union and communion to flourish. He offers us a vision of what is possible and then pledges his grace to help us live it.

> Thus *the marriage bond* has been established by God himself in such a way that a marriage concluded and consummated between baptized persons can never be dissolved. This bond, which results from the free human act of the spouses and their consummation of the marriage, is a reality, henceforth irrevocable, and gives rise to a covenant guaranteed by God's fidelity. (CCC, 1640)

God's faithfulness is the foundation of our faithfulness. We need to impart this vision to our children.

Marriage Under Attack

Our civilization is crumbling from within, and one of the reasons is no-fault divorce. Many celebrities seem to mock marriage, with multiple extravagant weddings, tabloid-reported affairs and public court battles for custody of children. Perhaps their struggle is greater than the average person's, as they try to balance fame, demanding careers and their private lives. Nevertheless, what started in Hollywood forty years ago is the norm today in many communities.

Even churchgoing people, including Catholics, now have as high a rate of divorce as non-Christians. Who is setting the example for whom? Rather than setting the standard for marriage the way God intended it, Christians are allowing the culture to influence how they make and break marriages.

Some people approach marriage the way they would a dress rehearsal—the lights, costumes and makeup for the production, including all lines memorized and delivered—rather than the finished star performance. "Starter marriage," a phrase made popular by Pamela Paul, refers to a childless union between people under thirty-five lasting less than five years.[1] Young couples, with an idealized view of marriage and a minimized view of divorce, "try" marriage.

Instead of catching a vision of the rights, responsibilities and risks of committing their lives to each other and seeing the act of marriage as the expression of that love in a new person, these couples focus exclusively on each other.

Separating the marriage act from marriage leads people to make poor choices for their spouses. Bioethicist Janet Smith comments, "When they do marry, they are often simply marrying a sexual partner that they have become used to. Sexual attraction and sexual compatibility become the chief foundation for relationships."[2] They do not want to fail, but they place such a premium on happiness that pain, difficulty, stress and challenge become excuses to cut their losses and move on.

If these people understood marriage as lifelong, would their choices be different? Frequently divorces for this age group become messy, with custody disputes—for pets, not for children—asset apportionments and debt assignments. The people hope to learn what will make a future marriage last.

No Divorces on Record

Can you imagine a town where no one has divorced? In Siroki-Brijeg, Herzegovina, population thirteen thousand, no divorces have been recorded, and no one remembers anyone getting divorced. These Christian people have suffered for their faith at the hands of the Turks and Communists; they know that salvation can only be found in the cross of Christ. "That is why they have indissolubly linked marriage with the Cross of Christ."[3]

When a priest in this town counsels a couple who desire marriage, he does not tell them that they have found the perfect mate but rather that they have found their cross to love, to treasure and to embrace. Their committed marital love will reflect the greatest love ever: Christ's cross. On the day they wed, the couple bring a crucifix to be blessed. During the exchange of vows, the bride lays her right hand on the crucifix, the groom covers her hand with his, and the priest places his stole over their joined hands. This is a witness to all that if they abandon each other, they abandon the cross. "And if they abandon the cross, they have nothing left. They have lost everything for they have abandoned Jesus."[4]

When they complete their vows, "The bride and groom do not then kiss each other, they rather kiss the cross."[5] Later this crucifix is placed in a prominent place in their home as a focal point for family prayer. Whenever the couple experience trouble—and they know trouble will come—they will go to the cross of Christ and pour out their hearts to him, for he alone can save them.

Divorce Is Against Natural Law

Since "the desire and ability of a man and a woman to form a lasting bond of love and life in marriage is written into their nature,"[6] it stands to reason that "*divorce* is a grave offense against the natural law" (*CCC*, 2384). Apart from grace a man and a woman can still make a commitment to faithfulness for the good of one another, their children and society at large.

Both of my paternal grandparents were children of divorce in the 1910s, which is hard to imagine. Though they were not Christians, they pledged to each other that, no matter what, they would remain married. On the basis of sheer willpower coupled with common sense and a lot of love, they provided for the emotional and psychological well-being of my father and uncle in many ways. Later, when they became Christians, they had supernatural resources of grace on which to build that commitment, making their marriage even sweeter and more precious.

Divorce Contravenes the Sacramental Sign

Christian marriage is a living sign pointing to the indissoluble bond between Christ as Bridegroom and the Church as bride. "Divorce does injury to the covenant of salvation, of which sacramental marriage is the sign,"[7] for how can we witness to our society about God's faithfulness if we are unfaithful to a spouse? Divorce is an offense against the dignity of marriage, and an attack on the sanctity of marriage.

Divorce Introduces Disorder

Divorce is a heartbreaking reality in many Christian families. Deeper than the disappointment of the failed marriage is the painful sense of loss.

> Divorce is immoral also because it introduces disorder into the family and into society. This disorder brings grave harm to the deserted spouse, to children traumatized by the separation of their parents and often torn between them, and because of its contagious effect which makes it truly a plague on society.[8]

How will grace build on nature when nature has been weakened and wounded through divorce, or when children's sense of peace and security is shattered? Grace can cover a multitude of sins, but children need parents to do all they can to bring healing and wholeness to marriage rather than strife, division and divorce.

Some argue that children are better off with divorced parents than with parents at war with each other. Is that the choice? Wouldn't children be still better off if parents called a truce and found help, through counseling and prayer, to remain together? Sure, that can be hard work, but a stable home and a peaceful environment are worth the sacrifices. Our prayer needs to be, "Lord, there's a way through this; please show us the way of escape that we may endure" (see 1 Corinthians 10:13).

Damage Done by Divorce

Divorce or its threat damages both ends of marriage: procreation and unity. The threat of divorce limits a couple's freedom to be open to life. Children of divorce suffer the loss of their parents' love for each other. This in turn becomes a loss of future siblings, a sadness and loneliness many children feel.

The threat of divorce contributes to independence rather than unity. Children of divorce no longer see their parents' selfless service for each other but instead see Mom and Dad attack each other and compete for the love and affection of their children. Since children are deprived of one parent at all times, they lose the sense of the protection, attention and guidance both parents would offer together.

Reconciliation Is Possible

Our God is a God of reconciliation. He delights in bringing good out of evil, bringing hope where there is despair. There is hope for reconciliation, even when a spouse "marries" after divorce outside the Church.

One college student shared her experience. Her father divorced her mother and "married" another woman. His older children never acknowledged the new "wife" as a legitimate parent, and they reminded their father that he was still married to their mom. Through many prayers, humiliations and acts of kindness and forgiveness, the couple reunited. The family was restored by the grace of God. Ongoing healing is still needed, for the period of the divorce was damaging; however, great blessing has come to this family. The restoration came before the children married, so the in-laws and grandchildren have experienced an intact family. This reconciliation continues to bless many people.

For couples who find it difficult to imagine reconciliation due to serious complications in their marriage, a marriage retreat called Retrouvaille and its follow-up sessions may offer an avenue of hope. Participants are restricted to those in serious situations. Contact www.retrouvaille.org for more information.

God's Beautiful Design for Marriage

Saint Augustine writes of the three goods of the sacrament of marriage. First, with every act of marriage open to life, a couple participates in generous fruitfulness. Their children are "begotten of love, tenderly cared for and educated in a religious atmosphere."[9] Second, a couple is faithful to each other exclusively. The sanctity of marriage precedes the sanctity of life. And third, a couple's indissoluble bond is a sign of their permanent union and their intimate communion.[10] This union is "the one blessing that was not forfeited by original sin or washed away in the flood."[11]

"Therefore a man leaves his father and his mother and clings to his wife, and they become one flesh. And the man and his wife were both naked, and were not ashamed" (Genesis 2:24–25). The union is actualized during the act of marriage, but it goes beyond a physical reality to the metaphysical reality that yields new persons: their children. Babies and intimate bonding between husband and wife result from living God's design for marriage. Children beautifully embody that union, as God enables husband and wife to be cocreators with him in making another human being.

Mutual Interior Formation

In addition to fruitfulness, faithfulness and unity, the sacrament of Matrimony gives a couple the graces necessary for the mutual interior transformation of each spouse. Each assists the other in becoming a saint.

[Marital love] holds pride of place in Christian marriage.... The deep attachment of the heart which is expressed in action...must have as its primary purpose that man and wife help each other day by day in forming and perfecting themselves in the interior life, so that through their partnership in life they may advance ever more and more in virtue, and above all that they may grow in true love toward God and their neighbor....

This mutual molding of husband and wife, this determined effort to perfect each other, can in a very real sense...be said to be the chief reason and purpose of matrimony...the blending of life as a whole and the mutual interchange and sharing thereof.[12]

This molding is a refining fire, which at times is painful but, with patience, is very fruitful. The prophet Malachi refers to the Lord as a refiner of silver (see Malachi 3:2–3). A silversmith holds the silver to be refined over the hottest part of the fire. He has to be watchful, so that all dross dissipates without destroying the silver. When is the silver fully refined? According to one craftsman, "When I see my image in it."

We will have times of refining, when we feel the heat of the fire. Let's remember that God holds us there to purify us, always watchful so that his image appears in us. This is true for us not only as individuals but also as a married couple who image the Trinity in our union.

Supporting Marriage

How can we support marriages in our local parish and community? How can we offer our young people more in the way of marriage preparation? What should we teach our children about courtship and marriage?

As much help as we may need from our priests and bishops, we also must assist them. Families need to minister to each other to bolster marriages and family life. "Young married couples should learn to accept willingly and make good use of the discreet, tactful and generous help offered by other couples that already have more experience of married and family life."[13] We need to nurture marital love in our marriage and in the marriages of those around us.

Couples who prepare for marriage can still find the year's ups and downs a great challenge. (It's similar to the difference between reading about birth and going through labor and delivery!) You can only prepare so much; and once you are in the midst of it, the preparation can feel inadequate. Sometimes it can be so overwhelming that one spouse feels like counseling is needed, but if they don't both agree, nothing may be done to get guidance when it could help the most.

I want to offer a challenge: What if the priest asks the couple at their last prenuptial meeting to sign up for two "check-up" appointments with him, say at four months and eight months post-wedding? (People do this all the time for doctors, dentists and orthodontists.) At the conclusion of the Mass closest to their one-year anniversary, the priest could offer congratulations and a small gift on behalf of the parish, thereby recognizing them and including the parish family in the celebration.

At my parents' fiftieth wedding anniversary celebration, I listed according to the five love languages the various ways my parents have assisted the married couples in our family. The underlying principle is that they have focused on our marriages first and the grandchildren second. They know their grandchildren will receive great blessing from parents who deeply love each other.

Besides our faith in Christ, I think the second biggest reason that there are twenty-six living grandchildren (and at least thirteen with the Lord) is that we have loving marriages. When marriages are happy, it is easier for couples to be open to life.

My parents are also aware that many of the pressures of life can create conflicts that make marriage and family life harder. They have sought to use their resources of time and money to bolster the core relationship of each family, and for that we will be eternally grateful. They have not had a lot of money through the years, but they have chosen to invest in our lives, especially enriching family life in wonderful ways.

So here is what my folks do. I hope this list inspires

you to prayerfully consider how you can encourage your children's marriages.

Quality Time

- Inviting us out to dinner as a couple and providing a sitter so that we can have uninterrupted adult conversation. Over holidays and on vacations, the couples in our family get together over a nice dinner while sitters care for the children. We catch up on each others' lives and find out how best to pray for each other. This facilitates quality time with siblings as well as Mom and Dad.

- Calling to share joys and sorrows, ending with Dad's asking, "Can I pray with you?"

- Praying daily for each child, in-law and grandchild by name.

- Entering into special celebrations of our children's Baptisms, Confirmations, championship games, recitals, concerts, award ceremonies, graduations and weddings.

- Making a yearly family vacation possible (through time shares), so that we can play and pray together. This includes sitters to ensure a vacation for all.

Physical Touch and Closeness

- Greeting us with hugs and kisses each time we see each other.

- Laying hands on our children in a prayer of blessing as a send-off from Papa.

- Giving back rubs.

- Providing thoughtful accommodations to facilitate a couple's intimacy.

Acts of Service

- Offering help with yard work, organizing, packing and unpacking, helping select wallpaper and paint, painting and baby-sitting so a couple can get away.

- Offering a week's worth of help with the arrival of every grandbaby—cooking, cleaning, caring for older children and walking with the baby in the wee hours of the morning so the parents can sleep.

Gift Giving

- Offering date money periodically, aware of the tensions that tight budgets can cause. Some years sending an Advent package of decorations. Other years, offering money for home improvements.

- Giving gifts primarily to the adults at Christmas. Their focus is on us, and our focus is on our children.

- Sharing books and other resources that are blessing their marriage.

Words of Affirmation

- Lavishing genuine compliments in person and in personal messages on birthday cards.

- Never playing favorite with a child, in-law or grandchild—ever.

- Calling us on Mother's Day and Father's Day to thank *us* for being good parents.

- Celebrating adult accomplishments—graduate degrees, promotions at work, books published and so on.

- Expressing thanks to in-laws, letting them know how they enrich everyone in the family.

- Celebrating children's talents with in-house shows at Christmas and on vacation.

- Speaking with respect and love about us to our children.

- Affirming our unity as a couple by maintaining loyalty to both of us.

- Displaying five-by-seven photos of twenty-six grandchildren and two greats (so far) in the front hall of their home.

- Expressing their love and affection in front of us, letting us know that the best is yet to come!

I am convinced that as we nurture the marriages in our families, we will unleash the power of grace in all of our lives more fully, for each faithful marriage strengthens others. Let's ask the Holy Spirit to give us the creativity we need, in the midst of whatever limitations we face, to be of genuine assistance to the marriages around us.

Be Not Afraid!

"Be not afraid!" The angels would not say that if there were no reason, on a human level, to be afraid. Here are a few examples.

The angel greets Zechariah, "Do not be afraid, Zechariah" (Luke 1:13), and then he tells him he will have a son, filled with the Holy Spirit, who will prepare the people for the Lord's anointed.

The angel Gabriel appears to Mary and says, "Do not be afraid, Mary, for you have found favor with God" (Luke 1:30), and then tells her she will conceive the Son of God.

Shortly thereafter the angel reveals God's plan to Joseph: "Joseph, son of David, do not fear to take Mary your wife, for that which is conceived in her is of the Holy Spirit" (Matthew 1:20).

Finally, to the shepherds the night of Jesus' birth, the angels echo the proclamation, "Be not afraid; for behold, I bring you good news of a great joy which will come to all the people" (Luke 2:10).

God's plan—for our lives, for our marriages, for our children—is more wonderful, challenging, joy-filled and sorrowful than we can imagine. We do not need to understand the fullness of his plan; we just need to imitate our Blessed Mother's response, "Behold, I am the handmaid of the Lord; let it be to me according to your word" (Luke 1:38).

King David prayed, "I sought the LORD and he answered me, / and delivered me from all my fears. ... The angel of the LORD encamps / around those who fear him, and delivers them" (Psalm 34:4, 7). Our fears are real. Yet when we bring them to God in prayer, they do not rob us of our joy and our peace.

Like the woman of faith described in Proverbs 31, we are to fear the Lord in love and obedience. We trust our heavenly Father, as his beloved daughters and sons, to provide the grace we need to live the vocation of marriage faithfully and fruitfully. Let's pray for each other, that through the witness of our marriages, many hearts will be drawn to the Bridegroom of our soul, Jesus, and to his bride, the Church.

Who Can Find a Good Wife?

Session One: Proverbs 31:10a

I. Why Proverbs 31? Circumstances behind this passage

II. Proverbs 31:10– 12

    A. What does it mean to be "good"?

    B. Proverbs 31:30

    C. Proverbs 18:22

III. Fear of the Lord

    A. Whom do we fear?

    B. Father and daughter or son, not master and slave

    C. How are we to fear the Lord? Obedience with joy —Psalm 112:1

    D. Blessings of the fear of the Lord—Psalm 103:17–18

        1. Mercy for generations—Luke 1:50

        2. Hope in his steadfast love—Psalm 147:11

        3. Beginning of knowledge—Proverbs 1:7

        4. Beginning of wisdom—Proverbs 9:10

        5. Confidence for husband; refuge for children —Proverbs 14:26

IV. God's love song for his people

    A. Israel created for his glory—Isaiah 43:1–4, 6–7

    B. We are chosen by Love for love—Ephesians 1:3–6

    C. We have a destiny—Ephesians 1:12

    D. God's plan includes our vocation: a particular call

V. Vocation = Call to holiness, single or married

    A. Spousal commitment and fruitfulness

    B. Something was not good—Genesis 2:18–23

    C. Two become one: change in relationship, role and potential

D. Primary channel of grace for each other

VI. Totally Yours, Jesus

    A. Jesus' summary of the law—Matthew 22:36–40, quoting Deuteronomy 6:4–6

    B. God's gifts

        1. Proverbs 19:14

        2. Proverbs 20:6–7

VII. Trust in the LORD

Far More Precious Than Jewels

Session Two: Proverbs 31:10b

I. What is more precious than jewels?—Proverbs 31:10–12
   A. Wisdom—Proverbs 3:15
   B. Knowledge—Proverbs 20:15
   C. A godly wife

II. What is the source of our value?
   A. World says: external things
      1. Youthfulness or beauty
      2. Fame for physical prowess, skill or talent
      3. Wealth
      4. Intelligence or career
      5. Marital status
   B. Romans 12:2: Do not be conformed to this world
      1. Complementary, not competitive—1 Timothy 5:8
      2. Focus is service—Titus 2:3–5
      3. Differences between men and women
         —Genesis 2:23
      4. Similarities between men and women
         a. Made in God's image—Genesis 1:27–28
         b. Need the promised Savior—Genesis 3:15
         c. Saved by Christ—Galatians 3:27–28

III. You were bought with a price.
   A. Temple of the Holy Spirit—1 Corinthians 6:19–20
   B. Called to be holy—1 Peter 1:15–16
   C. God's will is purity—1 Thessalonians 4:3

IV. Feel tarnished? Unfinished?
    —1 Corinthians 6:16
    A. Message of hope—Jeremiah 29:11
    B. Royal priesthood, holy nation, God's own people
       —1 Peter 2:9
    C. Gift of virginity; commitment of chastity

V. Forgiveness
    A. Sacrament of Confession
       1. Be specific: sorrow for sins
       2. Strength to resist temptation
       3. Penance: contribute to healing the brokenness
       4. Walk in forgiveness: believe God's Word
    B. Healing transformation; Saint Mary Magdalene
       —Luke 7:36–50
    C. Depends on God's faithfulness—1 John 1:9
    D. God is my honor—Psalms 62:5–7

VI. Pursue purity; flee fornication!—1 Corinthians 6:18
    A. Keep the fire in the fireplace—Proverbs 6:27–29
    B. Practical steps
    C. We are his workmanship—Ephesians 2:10

VII. Marriage to a nonbeliever
    A. Light and darkness—2 Corinthians 6:14
    B. Witness without words—1 Peter 3:1–2, 4
    C. Power of grace—1 Corinthians 7:14;
       2 Corinthians 5:17
    D. The Church's guidelines

The Heart of Her Husband Trusts in Her

Session Three: Proverbs 31:11a

I. The faithful one—Proverbs 31:10–12;
Lamentations 3:22–23

II. His heart = his well-being; track record of faithfulness
throughout courtship
   A. Privately she gives him for no cause for suspicion
   B. Publicly she is not a reproach to him

III. Missteps toward unfaithfulness—Proverbs 7:6–23
   A. Seductress's actions—Proverbs 5:3–4
   B. Man's missteps—Proverbs 5:23
   C. What a godly wife does
   D. What a godly husband does—Proverbs 5:18–19

IV. Marriage is the core relationship
   A. Competing needs
   B. At risk—1 Peter 5:8

V. Dealing with temptations to commit adultery
   A. Pray for wisdom—James 1:5
   B. Guard the inner sanctum

VI. How can we guard our marriage and build a foundation of trust?
   A. Thoughts: "Make love your aim"
      1. Prayer life—Galatians 5:22–23; thanksgiving
         —Philippians 4:6–7
      2. Purity of thought—Matthew 5:27–28
      3. Fill your mind with good thoughts
         —Philippians 4:8

      4. Thankful spirit: choose spouse daily
          —1 Thessalonians 5:16–18

B. Words: "Make love your aim"
    1. Prayer as a couple and as a family
    2. Slow to anger—James 1:19–20
    3. Communication skills; self-knowledge
        a. Personality inventories
        b. Understanding temperaments
        c. Birth order
        d. Five love languages
            i. Words of affirmation
            ii. Gift giving
            iii. Quality time
            iv. Physical touch and closeness
            v. Acts of service
    4. No lies, ever—Proverbs 12:22
    5. Practice discretion—Proverbs 17:9;
       1 Corinthians 13:7
    6. Contentment versus contentiousness
       —Proverbs 19:13; 21:9; 25:24; 27:15
        a. Fretful woman—Proverbs 21:19
        b. Quarrelsome man—Proverbs 26:21

C. Deeds: "Make love your aim."
    1. Practice the faith from a sincere heart
    2. Live chastity
        a. Modesty in dress
        b. Be affectionate with your spouse
           —1 Corinthians 7:5
        c. Marriage bed undefiled—Hebrews 13:4
        d. Guard marriage in relation to friendships
    3. Deal with temptations that arise
       —1 Corinthians 10:13
        a. Stop
        b. Go to Confession
        c. Cut off attachments
        d. Avoid the near occasions of sin

      e. Eliminate reminders

      f. Talk to spouse

      g. Build accountability

      h. Break old habits and foster new ones

      i. Marriage Encounter or a Retrouvaille Retreat

VII. How does a godly woman build her house?
   —Proverbs 14:1

He Will Have No Lack of Gain

Session Four: Proverbs 31:11b

I. Covenant of marriage—Proverbs 31:10–12
    A. Covenant versus contract
    B. Total gift of self to other—Mark 8:34–35
    C. Healthy interdependence
II. No lack of gain in finances
    A. Stewardship
    B. Tithe—Malachi 3:8–10
    C. Budget
    D. Interests of others—Philippians 2:1–4
III. No lack of gain in terms of children
    A. Blessed to be a blessing—Genesis 1:26–28
    B. Children are the supreme gift of marriage
    C. Nurture life
IV. No lack of gain due to her ministry of presence
    A. Power play
    B. Time spender rather than a wage earner
V. No lack of gain because he values what God values in a woman
    A. Transformed thinking on life—Romans 12:2
    B. No cafeteria of values—John 8:31–32
VI. Queen of the realm, heart of the home
    A. Home a sanctuary, a haven, a harbor, a place of peace
    B. Home a place of beauty and order
    C. A helper fit for him—Genesis 2:18

VI. Marriage: the big picture
  A. Mystery: marriage as witness to Christ and the Church—Ephesians 5:31–32; Genesis 2:24, quoted by Jesus in Matthew 19:5
  B. God is the author of marriage—Ephesians 3:14–15
  C. Order of Authority
    1. Pre-Fall Adam is head of the human family—Genesis 2:23
    2. Post-Fall Adam is still head but conflict ensues—Genesis 3:16
    3. The mystery of authority
      a. Trinity: functional subordination without diminution of any Person
      b. Functional subordination within family without diminution of any person
    4. Love and respect—Ephesians 5:21–28, 33
      a. Both subject to Christ
      b. Husband is head of the home; wife submits to him
      c. Husband is servant leader like Christ, loves his bride
      d. Wife respects husband: marry one worthy of trust!
      e. Servant leadership—Matthew 20:25–28
      f. Beloved unbeliever?—1 Peter 3:1–2
  D. Order of Love
    1. Wife is the heart of the home: healthy interdependence
    2. She is first in the order of love
    3. She has derivative authority as queen alongside the king
    4. Wise man listens to her heart: pulse on home and children
    5. Each is deferential to the other, seeking harmony
    6. She cares for his needs: body, name, family, estate

She Does Him Good and Not Harm

Session Five: Proverbs 31:12a

I. "Doing good" flows from a heart for God
—Proverbs 31:10–12
   A. Trust in God and then act—Psalm 37:3–5
   B. Heart is source for good or evil—Matthew 12:34–35

II. She does him good by embracing commitment in marriage.
   A. Marriage is a public and permanent pledge.
   B. The bond of marriage is not bondage
   C. God is the Author of marriage
   D. Marriage is a source of grace—John 15:5

III. She does him good by valuing the act of marriage
   A. Sex is _____
   B. Our bodies are consecrated to sacred use
   C. Giving the gift of self; receiving the gift of your spouse and the gift of children

IV. How do you enter into a licit marriage?
   A. Free consent
   B. Open to life
   C. We are the ministers of the sacrament: channels of grace

V. To be your loving and faithful wife in joy and in sorrow
   A. Compassion—Romans 12:15
   B. Bear each other's burdens—Galatians 6:2
      1. Grieve differently
      2. Listen to dreams
      3. Build bridges with each other's families

VI. In sickness and in health
    A. Illness and disability; prepare for old age
        1. 1 Corinthians 13:5
        2. Job's wife—Job 2:7–10
    B. Our sufferings united to Christ's—Colossians 1:24
        1. Temptations toward the end of life
    C. Nutrition: serve it with love—Proverbs 15:17
        1. Pleasant words help digestion—Proverbs 16:24
        2. Share good things—Proverbs 15:30

VII. For richer, for poorer
    A. Contentment versus the root of all evil
        —1 Timothy 6:6–10
    B. Love God and use money—Philippians 4:11–13

VIII. For better, for worse
    A. Strong bear with weak—Romans 15:1
    B. Idiosyncracies: note preferences; make adjustments
    C. Love is not irritable or resentful
        —1 Corinthians 13:5
        1. Hormone shifts: PMS, pregnancy, menopause
        2. Life's irritations

IX. Anger
    A. A troublesome emotion—Proverbs 15:18
    B. No harshness toward a wife—Colossians 3:19
    C. A powerful emotion—Ephesians 4:26–27, quoting Psalm 4:4
    D. Passion needing self-control: fire

X. How do we express anger?
    A. When words are many—Proverbs 10:19
    B. Avoid quarrels—Proverbs 15:1
    C. Self-control—Proverbs 16:32
    D. Watch your associates—Proverbs 22:24–25
    E. Anger leads to a sense of insecurity
        —Proverbs 25:28

XI. Desire and nurture unity
    A. Keeping short accounts
    B. Tool: Anger Ladder

C. Kindness nurtures repentance and change
   —Romans 2:4

D. He is able!—Ephesians 3:20–21

All the Days of Her Life

Session Six: Proverbs 31:12b

I. All the days before marriage: honorable courtship
   A. Pursue purity
   B. Time of preparation
II. All the days during marriage
   A. Lifelong commitment, like Christ toward his spouse
   B. We guard our marriage in chastity
   C. We embrace our spouse in generous fruitfulness
      —CCC, 8
III. All the days following death or divorce
   A. Protector of widows—Psalms 68:5; 146:9
   B. Free to remarry after death—1 Corinthians 7:39
IV. God hates divorce—Malachi 2:13–16
   A. Faithlessness to wife ruins your marriage and your relationship with God
   B. God's desire = godly offspring; assumes faithfulness
V. The Pharisees' trap
   A. Matthew 19:1–3
      1. Controversy dialogue set in King Herod's territory
      2. Two current schools of thought and Jesus' unexpected response
   B. Matthew 19:4–6
      1. Jesus teaches the Pharisees Genesis
      2. No one can separate what God has joined
      3. Indissolubility reflects God's love for his people
VI. What did Moses teach?
   A. Pharisees' objection—Matthew 19:7–8

B. Allowance for hardness of heart
—Deuteronomy 24:1–4

VII. What did Jesus teach about remarriage after divorce?
 A. No exception—Luke 16:18
 B. No exception—Mark 10:11–12
 C. An exception clause—Matthew 19:9
  1. Cannot contradict other teachings of Jesus
  2. *Pornea*: grounds for annulment
   —1 Corinthians 5:1–2
  3. Possible interpretations

VIII. What did Saint Paul teach about divorce?
 A. Separation or reconciliation—1 Corinthians 7:10–11
 B. Beware of adulterous actions—Romans 7:2–3

IX. Witness of the disciples
 A. The disciples get it; it's a hard saying
  —Matthew 19:10, 11
 B. Jesus confirms indissolubility
 C. Jesus teaches about celibacy: also a hard saying
 D. No easy choice to follow Jesus: It means there's
  a cross!

X. Witness of the Church through the ages
 A. Compared to other religions
 B. Universal teaching until sixteenth century
 C. Franciscan martyrs of Georgia: issue of
  indissolubility
 D. Fears related to divorce

XI. Annulments
 A. Appeal to a Church court: valid, sacramental
  marriage occurred?
 B. Process of annulment
 C. Honorable courtship is possible following
  annulment
 D. If marriage is invalid for some reason, person is free
  to marry

XII. Marriage, in summary
 A. From the beginning

   B.   God is a faithful husband
   C.   Jesus' first miracle
   D.   The end of time is a wedding feast
   E.   Mutual interior formation
XIII. Be not afraid
   A.   Luke 1:13
   B.   Luke 1:30
   C.   Matthew 1:20
   D.   Luke 2:10
   E.   Psalm 34:4, 7

Session One: Who Can Find a Good Wife?

1. How is faith the foundation of my marriage?

2. What does the "fear of the Lord" mean to me? What is the difference between the kind of fear that leads to despair and the fear of the Lord that brings hope? Do I view God as a loving Father, whom I want to please because I value my relationship to him, or as a demanding boss, who might "fire" me if he's displeased with me?

3. Do I see myself as a grace-gift from the Lord to my spouse? Do I view my spouse as a conquest or a gift?

4. Is my spouse's primary relationship with God or with me? Am I keeping the proper order of relationships: God, spouse, children, friends...?

5. How am I the primary channel of grace for my spouse?

6. Are there ways I am a roadblock to grace? How can I keep the channel of grace unclogged?

7. What does it mean to be chosen by God before the foundation of the world (see Ephesians 1:4)?

8. "Mature womanhood is spousal commitment and motherhood." How can this be applied to all: single, consecrated and married?

9. Do I view children as a gift from God or as a hindrance to my chosen lifestyle? How does my spouse view children?

10. For those not yet married: What essential preparations should I make for this vocation? For those who are married: How did I prepare, and how do I wish I had prepared?

11. What did the "Totally Yours" skit say to me? What does the lordship of Jesus Christ mean for my marriage? What areas of my life do I need to surrender to God?

12. If I want to grow in my faith, I must do more than know facts about God: I must know him, love him, enjoy him. What are some parallels between growing in intimacy with a beloved and growing in intimacy with the Lord?

How do I develop a relationship...

...with someone?	...with God?
a. Spend time together alone	Prayer
b. Spend time together with others	
c. Eat together	
d. Write letters to him	
e. Read letters written to me	
f. Apologize	
g. Share with others the wonderful things happening	
h. Stand up for each other in loyalty	
i. Do little things for each other	
j. Be there for each other through difficulties	
k. Seek guidance from others	

Session Two: She Is Far More Precious Than Jewels

1. Do I know how precious I am in God's sight as his beloved child?

2. Who or what determines my sense of worth?

3. Read Romans 12:2. What does it mean to not be conformed to this world?

4. How can I utilize the sacrament of Confession to clear the channel of grace in my life? What can I do when I have guilt feelings after I have confessed?

5. How can my spouse and I encourage each other in the discipline of Confession, and what difference can that make in our marriage? Did our parents help us to establish a habit of going to Confession? How can we help our children go to Confession on a regular basis?

6. Who are role models for me and my spouse? What are their qualities I want to emulate?

7. Why are differences between men and women complementary rather than competitive? What gifts, abilities, skills and interests do my spouse

and I bring to our marriage? How will we use these gifts to strengthen each other and our marriage?

8. What responsibility does a man have according to 1 Timothy 5:8?

9. With a focus on service to the family, how does the man's role as provider and the woman's role as homemaker strengthen the family? Do I value these roles?

10. For those not yet married: How am I preparing for the responsibility of my role and for supporting my future spouse's role?

11. What value do I place on purity? Is my spouse keeping our intimacy pure? For those not yet married: Does the person I date encourage purity?

12. Is our intimate relationship based on God-given desire or lust? If lust, how can we refocus our relationship? How can we help our children discern between lust and love?

13. Cohabitation is the attempt to practice married life without the grace of marriage and without the graces available in Confession and the Eucharist. It is destructive to a relationship at many levels and to the couple's witness. Have I rejected this "worldly wisdom"? Can I explain to others why this is a false path for true love?

14. What might my spouse and I do to let people know we have a Catholic Christian marriage?

15. What does this statement mean: "My husband [wife] is not an obstacle to my sanctification; he [she] is part of my sanctification"?

16. What can I say to a friend or a child who is considering marrying a non-Christian?

17. If my spouse is an unbeliever or has weak faith, how can I make Christ the foundation of our marriage?

18. How can we help our sons value a godly woman?

Session Three: The Heart of Her Husband Trusts in Her

1. How can flirting before marriage contribute to unhealthy patterns of relating in marriage?

2. How do I relate with my friends of the opposite sex? Does change need to occur?

3. What are some innocent acts that could lead to sin? How does this relate to the idea of the "near occasion of sin"? For instance, is it OK to go to lunch with coworkers of the opposite sex? Under what conditions?

4. How is pornography destructive to a relationship? Why is it wrong? What keeps the marriage bed undefiled?

5. What insight have I gained from Proverbs 7 regarding the threat of adultery?

6. Instead of becoming anxious or jealous, how can I assist my spouse or future spouse in marital faithfulness?

7. How can we develop a prayer life as a couple? Do we know someone who can be a good example in that area?

8. Is there one new idea I want to implement from the suggestions about building the foundation of trust through my thoughts, words and deeds?

9. Do the things I watch, read and think about help me keep my marriage holy and my heart for my spouse?

10. Is our relationship primarily sexual in nature, or is it built primarily on friendship? If it is primarily sexual, what could we do to build up other areas that may be lacking?

11. In the area of communication skills, how am I different from my spouse? How do we differ in temperament, personality, birth order and love languages? With whom can I share communication difficulties I am having with my spouse or my intended, so that we can get help without harming our relationship?

12. Have I seen my parents or another married couple honor each other in ways that I hope we emulate?

Session Four: And He Will Have No Lack of Gain

1. What transitions have I made in marriage from independence to healthy interdependence? What was my biggest challenge?

2. How can I better assist my spouse in the area of finances? Am I disciplined in my spending habits? If not, how can I gain greater self-control in this area?

3. Regarding a budget, is the greater difficulty setting it up or managing it?

4. Do I consider tithing important? Why or why not?

5. Do I think it is more valuable for a wife and mom to be a time spender or a wage earner?

6. What does it mean to have a ministry of presence in the home?

7. How have attitudes from older relatives influenced my openness to life?

8. How do I feel about welcoming children into the world? Does my spouse share my perspective regarding openness to life?

9. What does "Children reveal the life-giving power of love" mean to me? What lessons of "littleness" have my children taught me?

10. How can I make my home a place of welcome, peace and order?

11. What style of leadership have I experienced from my father?

12. Did my mother give me a good example of godly submission? What is the difference between a woman who feels like a doormat and a woman who feels like queen of the realm under the king?

13. What do I think of the idea of the man as the head of the home and the woman as the heart of the home?

14. Does the "order of authority" threaten me? What practical steps can I take to build trust in my spouse so that his or her role is a blessing to our family?

15. What are specific ways I communicate respect toward my spouse? Do I value what God values?

16. For wives: How can I encourage my husband to lead spiritually, even if I am the more spiritual one of the two of us?

17. For husbands: Do I hold my authority under Christ's authority? How can I lead my family spiritually?

18. How can we teach our sons to be spiritual leaders someday in their homes?

19. Is there a couple who might be good mentors for us? How might we approach them?

Session Five: She Does Him Good, and Not Harm

1. What example or thought has strengthened my understanding of the wedding vow "in joy and in sorrow"? "In sickness and in health"? "For richer or for poorer"? "For better or for worse"?

2. Marriage is "the art of coming alongside one another." What does this mean?

3. Money is neither moral nor immoral: We can use it for good or for evil. How has money had an impact on our marriage?

4. Are we of one mind on finances, or are they a constant source of tension? Have financial concerns been detrimental to our family peace? How can this be resolved? What attitude shifts do I need to make? What are my top three concerns regarding finances? How can I constructively address these concerns with my spouse?

5. What do I do to overcome my difficulties related to hormonal changes?

6. What are the qualities that should characterize our family as we try to imitate the Holy Family?

7. Have I worked out rules of conflict with my spouse? Do I follow them?

8. How might the Anger Ladder be a helpful tool in my marriage and family? Can I see what steps I need to take to improve how I express anger? Can this be a helpful tool for our older children?

9. How was anger expressed in my home of origin? In my spouse's home?

10. What patterns from our families do I want to imitate? What patterns do I want to change?

11. What is the difference between peace at any price and true peace?

12. What does it mean for women to be the guardian of relationships? How does this fit a wife's role in the "order of love" in the family?

13. "Don't do married things before you are married." What does this mean regarding cohabitation? Why is it unwise to disobey God in this area? How can I correct problems that disobedience may have caused or may still be causing?

14. What does it mean to refer to sex as holy? Does the Catholic teaching on marriage interfere or complement love and sex? Can I explain this to others?

Session Six: All the Days of Her Life

1. How can an unmarried person honor a future spouse?

2. For the widowed or divorced: In what ways can I continue to honor this person?

3. What does Jesus mean when he says that man cannot separate what God has joined?

4. What difference does Jesus' teaching on divorce make? How is Jesus' teaching on divorce different from Jewish tradition?

5. Why is monogamy (one man, one woman in marriage) essential in reflecting God's relationship to us?

6. What in the talk on the indissolubility of marriage touched me? How do I view indissolubility?

7. How has the modern view toward divorce influenced our thoughts on having children?

8. How do children benefit from our commitment to our marriage?

9. What does the true story about no divorces in a town mean to me?

10. For a wife: Since I am a "helper fit for him" by God's design, how might I assist my spouse in growing in virtue to be a courageous and holy man of God?

11. For a husband: How can I enable my wife to help me to be the man of God she needs me to be?

12. How can we encourage stronger marriages in our parish?

13. What can my spouse and I do to communicate these ideas to young couples preparing for marriage?

14. How can we discourage divorce? How can we encourage a different mind-set than "starter marriages?"

15. What can we do to nurture the core relationship of marriage in our family?

16. How has this study changed my thinking about the Lord? Myself? My marriage?

Session One: Who Can Find a Good Wife?

1. How can faith be the foundation of our marriage?

2. How has God led us together?

3. Do I see myself as a grace-gift to my future spouse?

4. How am I preparing to be the primary channel of grace for my spouse?

5. Are there ways I may be a roadblock to grace? How can I keep the channel of grace unclogged?

6. Is the person I am marrying someone I can live with for the rest of my life without changing him or her?

7. When I think about marriage, do I fear the loss of freedom, independence, control over finances or some other thing I value?

8. What do I think about the idea that God chose me, my spouse and our children from before the foundation of the world?

9. Do I see marriage and the commitment to parenthood as inseparably linked?

10. In regard to the "Totally Yours" skit, what does the lordship of Jesus Christ mean for my marriage? How do I understand stewardship in marriage?

11. I have developed my relationship to my future spouse in a variety of ways. What parallels do I see between growing in intimacy with a beloved and growing in intimacy with the Lord?

To develop an intimate relationship...

...with someone	...with God
a. Spend time together alone	Prayer
b. Spend time together with others	
c. Eat together	
d. Write letters to your beloved	
e. Read letters written to you by your beloved	
f. Apologize	
g. Share with others the wonderful things happening	
h. Stand up for each other in loyalty	
i. Do little things for each other	
j. Be there for each other through difficulties	
k. Receive guidance from others	

Session Two: She Is Far More Precious Than Jewels

1. What are some of the issues and mixed messages on marriage I see in the media that are destructive to marriage?

2. Who is a role model for me as a wife or a husband? What are the qualities I would like to emulate?

3. Why are differences between men and women complementary rather than competitive?

4. What are the gifts, abilities, skills and interests that each of us brings to our marriage? How will these strengthen us and our marriage?

5. How does the man's role as provider and the woman's role as homemaker strengthen the family?

6. Do I value these roles?

7. How am I preparing for the responsibility of my role and for supporting my spouse's role?

8. How can each of us encourage the other in the discipline of Confession, and what difference can that make in our marriage?

9. Is each of us guarding the other's purity? Have we set clear boundaries, and are both of us working to maintain them? Is anyone holding us accountable? If not, is there someone who could?

10. Cohabitation is the attempt to practice married life without the grace of marriage and any other graces a couple could receive through Confession and the Eucharist. It is destructive on many levels to the couple and their witness. Have I rejected this "worldly wisdom"? Can I explain to others why this is a false path to true love?

11. What might we do to let people know we are preparing for a Catholic Christian marriage?

Session Three: The Heart of Her Husband Trusts in Her

1. How can flirting before marriage contribute to unhealthy patterns of relating?

2. Have I noticed a change in my friendships with the opposite sex? Does change need to occur?

3. What are some innocent acts that could lead to sin? How does this relate to the idea of the "near occasion of sin"?

4. How is pornography destructive to a relationship? Why is it wrong?

5. What advice have I gained from Proverbs 7 regarding the threat of adultery?

6. Instead of becoming anxious or jealous, how can I assist my future spouse in marital faithfulness?

7. How can we develop a prayer life as a couple? Do we know a couple who can help us in this area?

8. In the area of communication skills, how am I different from my future spouse? How do we differ in temperament, personality, birth order and love languages?

9. Have I seen my parents or another married couple honor each other in ways that I hope we can emulate?

10. With whom can I share communication difficulties I am having with my future spouse, so that we can get help without harming our relationship?

Session Four: And He Will Have No Lack of Gain

1. What transitions am I making from independence to healthy interdependence?

2. Are there specific areas where I am challenged to extend trust to my intended?

3. Am I already using a budget? What is the toughest challenge for me with budgeting: setting it up, managing it or something else?

4. Was I taught about tithing from my parents? Do I tithe? Do I plan to tithe?

5. Have the attitudes of older adults in my family influenced my openness to life? How do I see children? Am I open to life?

6. Do I think it is valuable for a wife and mom to be a time spender rather than a wage earner?

7. What does a wife's ministry of presence in the home mean to me?

8. How can we together make a home a place of welcome, peace and order for our family and others whom we welcome?

9. What style of leadership have I experienced from my father?

10. Have I seen good examples of godly submission worth emulating? What is the difference between a woman being a doormat and a woman being queen of the realm under the king?

11. For the future wife: What are specific ways I communicate respect toward my future spouse?

12. For the future husband: How can I offer spiritual leadership to my wife and family, even if my fiancée seems to be the more spiritual one of the two of us?

13. What do I think of the idea of the man as the head of the home and the woman as the heart of the home?

14. Do we know a couple who might be good mentors for us? How might we approach them?

Session Five: She Does Him Good, and Not Harm

1. "Don't do married things before you are married." What does this mean to you?

2. What are the dangers of cohabitation before marriage?

3. Why do we refer to sex as holy?

4. When I prepare to say my marriage vow, what does "I do" mean in the following areas:

   "In joy and in sorrow"?

   "In sickness and in health"?

   "For richer or for poorer"?

   "For better or for worse"?

   "As long as we both shall live"?

5. Colossians 3:12–25 is a suggested New Testament reading at weddings, and it is read on the Feast of the Holy Family. What are the qualities that should characterize our family as we try to imitate the Holy Family?

6. What rules of conflict are important to me?

7. Does the Anger Ladder make sense? Where do I see myself on it?

8. What steps do I need to take to improve how I express anger?

9. How was anger expressed in my home as I was growing up? Is this a pattern I want to imitate?

10. What is the difference between peace at any price and true peace?

Session Six: All the Days of Her Life

1. How can an unmarried person honor a future spouse?

2. For the widowed or divorced: In what ways can I continue to honor my late or former spouse?

3. What does Jesus mean when he says that man cannot separate what God has joined?

4. How is Jesus' teaching on divorce different from Jewish tradition in the Old Testament?

5. What in the talk on the indissolubility of marriage touched me?

6. How can we encourage a different mind-set than "starter marriages"?

7. Why is monogamy (one man, one woman in marriage) essential in reflecting God's relationship to us?

8. How has the modern view permitting divorce influenced our thoughts on having children?

9. How do children benefit from our commitment to our marriage?

10. How can a parish support us in our marriage? Do we feel supported?

11. How can our engagement be a witness to others who are approaching engagement?

12. "You have not found the perfect spouse. You have found your cross to be embraced, carried, and treasured." What do I think of this statement?

13. What does the true story about the town with no divorces mean to me?

14. How has this study contributed to our preparation for marriage?

Bibliography

Bennett, Art and Laraine. *The Temperament God Gave You: The Classic Key to Knowing Yourself, Getting Along with Others, and Growing Closer to the Lord.* Manchester, N.H.: Sophia, 2005.

Berry, Jo. *Beloved Unbeliever: Loving Your Husband into Faith.* Grand Rapids: Zondervan, 1981.

Blue, Ronald. *Master Your Money.* Nashville: Thomas Nelson, 1991.

Campbell, Ross. *Kids in Danger: Disarming the Destructive Power of Anger in Your Child.* Wheaton, Ill.: Victor, 1995.

Chapman, Gary. *The Five Love Languages: How to Express Heartfelt Commitment to Your Mate.* Chicago: Northfield, 1995.

De Sales, Francis. *Introduction to the Devout Life.* New York: Dutton, 1961.

Fernandez, Francis. *In Conversation with God.* London: Scepter, 1997.

Hahn, Kimberly. *Life-Giving Love: Embracing God's Beautiful Design for Marriage.* Cincinnati: Servant, 2001.

Hahn, Scott and Leon J. Suprenant, eds. *Catholic for a Reason: Scripture and the Mystery of Marriage and Family Life.* Steubenville, Ohio: Emmaus Road, 2007.

Leman, Kevin. *The New Birth Order Book: Why You Are the Way You Are.* Grand Rapids: Revell, 1998.

Lenahan, Phil. *7 Steps to Becoming Financially Free: A Catholic Guide to Managing Your Money.* Huntington, Ind.: Our Sunday Visitor, 2006.

McCluskey, Christopher and Rachel. *When Two Become One: Achieving Sexual Intimacy in Marriage.* Grand Rapids: Revell, 2004.

Pierlot, Holly. *A Mother's Rule of Life: How to Bring Order to Your Home and Peace to Your Soul.* Manchester, N.H.: Sophia, 2004.

Rainey, Dennis. *Lonely Husbands, Lonely Wives: Rekindling Intimacy in Every Marriage.* Dallas, Tex.: Word, 1989.

Von Hildebrand, Alice. *By Grief Refined: Letters to a Widow.* Steubenville, Ohio: Franciscan University Press, 1994.

————. *By Love Refined: Letters to a Young Bride.* Manchester, N.H.: Sophia, 1989.

Wood, Stephen. *The ABCs of Choosing a Good Husband: How to Find and Marry a Great Guy.* Port Charlotte, Fla.: Family Life, 2001.

————. *The ABCs of Choosing a Good Wife: How to Find and Marry a Great Girl.* Port Charlotte, Fla: Family Life, 2007.

Organizations

Engaged Encounter: www.engagedencounter.org

Marriage Encounter: www.wwme.org

> Worldwide Marriage Encounter, Inc.
> 2210 East Highland Ave., Suite 106,
> San Bernardino, CA 92404-4666
> 909-863-9963

Retrouvaille: www.retrouvaille.org, 800-470-2230

St. Joseph's Covenant Keepers: www.dads.org

> Family Life Center
> 2130 Wade Hampton Blvd.
> Greenville, SC 29615
> 864-268-6730

St. Paul Center for Biblical Theology:
www.salvationhistory.com

> St. Paul Center
> 2228 Sunset Blvd., Suite 2A
> Steubenville, OH 43952
> 740-264-9535

Notes

Chapter Two: Trust in the Lord

1. Josemaría Escrivá, *Christ Is Passing By* (Princeton, N.J.: Scepter, 1974), p. 49.

Chapter Three: What Really Counts

1. See Pope John Paul II, *Mulieris Dignitatem,* Apostolic Letter on the Dignity and Vocation of Women, August 15, 1988, no. 17; and Letter to Women, June 29, 1995, www.vatican.va.

2. Mary Beth Bonacci, *Real Love* (San Francisco: Ignatius, 1996), p. 145.

Chapter Four: A Woman of Worth

1. Translation found in the *New Scofield Reference Edition* of the Bible.

2. See Vatican II, *Gaudium et Spes,* Pastoral Constitution on the Church in the Modern World, no. 48.

3. This phrase is found in the *English Standard Version* and the *King James Version.*

Chapter Six: How to Build Trust Daily

1. Fulton J. Sheen, *Three to Get Married* (Princeton, N.J.: Scepter, 1996).

2. For information on Catholic Engaged Encounter, go to www.engagedencounter.org/. For information on Marriage Encounter, write Worldwide Marriage Encounter, Inc., 2210 East Highland Ave., Suite 106, San Bernardino, CA 92404-4666. Phone 909-863-9963. E-mail office@wwme.org.

3. The Myer-Briggs Personality Inventory is an outstanding resource. See www.PersonalityPathways.com.

4. Art and Laraine Bennett, *The Temperament God Gave You: The Classic Key to Knowing Yourself, Getting Along with Others, and Growing Closer to the Lord* (Manchester, N.H.: Sophia, 2005); also Florence Littaur, *Your Personality Tree* (Nashville: W Publishing Group, 1986).

5. Kevin Leman. *The Birth Order Book: Why You Are the Way You Are* (Grand Rapids: Revell, 2004).

6. Gary Chapman, *The Five Love Languages: How to Express Heartfelt Commitment to Your Mate* (Chicago: Northfield, 1992).

7. The next volume in this series will cover this area in greater detail.

8. Retrouvaille: A Lifeline for Married Couples. For more information call 800-470-2230 or go to www.retrouvaille.org.

Chapter Seven: Complementarity

1. *Mulieris Dignitatem,* no. 5, referring to *Lumen Gentium,* no. 36.

Chapter Eight: Healthy Interdependence

1. Committee on Liturgy, National Council of Catholic Bishops, quoted by John Kippley in *Marriage Is for Keeps* (Cincinnati: The Foundation for the Family, Inc., 1993), p. 128.

2. Leo XIII Arcanum, n. 11, www.vatican.va/holy_father/leo_xiii/encyclicals/documents. In his encyclical *On Christian Marriage* n. 29, Pope Pius XI quotes Leo XIII, affirming the order of authority within marriage, www.papalencyclicals.net/Pius11/P11CASTI.HTM.

3. Pope Pius XII, *Casti Connubii*, Encyclical on Christian Marriage, December 31, 1930, no. 27.

Chapter Ten: Conflict Resolution

1. Gary Chapman and Ross Campbell, *The Five Love Languages of Children* (Chicago: Moody, 1997), p. 155.

Chapter Eleven: Faithful Now and Always

1. Francis de Sales, *Introduction to the Devout Life* (New York: Vintage, 2002), p. 183.

2. Pope John Paul II, *Familiaris Consortio,* Apostolic Exhortation on the Role of the Family in the Modern World, November 22, 1981, no. 20.

3. *Ignatius Press Study Bible, Matthew,* p. 51.

4. For more information see the *New Catholic Encyclopedia* and the *Catechism of the Catholic Church*, 1625–1629.

Chapter Twelve: The Sanctity of Marriage

1. Pamela Paul, *The Starter Marriage and the Future of Matrimony* (New York: Random House, 2002), p. xiii.

2. Janet Smith, "Natural Law and Sexual Ethics," good-morals.org/smith5.htm (2000).

3. Sister Emmanuel, "The Key to No Divorce," ecatholic-churches.com.

4. Sister Emmanuel.

5. Sister Emmanuel.

6. United States Conference of Catholic Bishops, "Married Love and the Gift of Life," issued November 14, 2006.

7. "Married Love and the Gift of Life."

8. "Married Love and the Gift of Life."

9. Augustine, quoted in Pope Pius XII, *Casti Connubii,* no. 10.

10. Augustine, quoted in *Casti Connubii,* no. 10.

11. This taken from the first nuptial blessing in the Rite of Marriage, quoted by John Kippley in *Marriage Is for Keeps,* p. 145.

12. *Casti Connubii*, nos. 23, 24.

13. *Familiaris Consortio,* no. 69.